GIMME FIVE

GIMME FIVE

SHASHI K. GULHATI

BLOOMSBURY
NEW DELHI • LONDON • OXFORD • NEW YORK • SYDNEY

First published, 2016

BLOOMSBURY PUBLISHING INDIA PVT. LTD.
New Delhi London Oxford New York Sydney

ISBN: 978-93-85936-25-8

10 9 8 7 6 5 4 3 2 1

Published by Bloomsbury Publishing India Pvt. Ltd.
DDA Complex LSC, Building No. 4, 2nd Floor
Pocket 6 & 7, Sector C
Vasant Kunj, New Delhi 110070

Laser Typeset by FORTUNE GRAPHICS, Naraina, New Delhi

Printed and bound in India by Thomson Press India Ltd.

Contents

The Inspiration

THE first few pages of a book usually have the sections: Acknowledgements, Foreword, Preface, Prologue, etc. For this Book, in lieu of these sections, I place before you 'The Inspiration'. Why this Book? Where did the idea originate from? What is it about? Where did the inspiration come from? Who inspired me? The story is personal, so please indulge me.

I graduated and then specialized and became an engineer through study abroad and then came back home to India hoping to make myself useful. It did not take long to figure out that working as an engineer, I would be useful but my reach would be infinitesimal. An individual's reach would be tiny in a country as large as ours – so I decided to make use of the multiplier effect and decided to become an engineer-educationist.

I joined the Indian Institute of Technology (IIT) at Delhi and that gave me an opportunity to be an engineer through consulting and be a teacher actively helping bright students to become good and great engineers and do their bit for the country – the greater the number of 'bits', the more would be their cumulative usefulness.

I had studied to become an engineer but not to educate others. As luck would have it, I got married to Rashmi, an educationist, and slowly but steadily began to learn the skills of teaching from her.

The first lesson loomed up after Rashmi happened to attend a lecture on a general topic delivered by a colleague of mine at IIT. After the lecture was over, Rashmi expressed her view to me that the lecturer was talking to himself and making no effort to effectively communicate the content of his lecture to those who had come to listen to him. In the days that followed, I went and sat in on lectures by many of my other colleagues and, sure enough, it was amply evident that we all needed to learn to communicate better.

I studied communication theory and then shared it with my colleagues. To delve further into the subject, I went to a university in U.S.A. to teach a summer course on Effective Communication and in the process honed in more on the subject. I returned and delivered a series of special lectures to students at IIT to help them in developing this soft skill.

Rashmi decided to attend a special course on script writing conducted by the National Council for Educational Research and Training. I kept in touch with what she was learning and soon realized that at IIT we were not taking any advantage of the new technology, although some of it was already available for use by teachers. I proceeded to prepare a video programme on how to conduct a particular laboratory test. It was an eye-opener. The video programme could be so effectively used to teach students in other colleges that may not have the equipment or the faculty with sufficient expertise. I then proposed to IIT to focus on using and developing such new technologies and pursued that goal until IIT set up the Centre for Educational Technology.

During her Bachelor of Education course, Rashmi had specialized in 'pre-school' education. Before getting married and soon thereafter, she taught at leading play schools in Delhi. She just loved her interaction with children and each day, when she returned from school, she had inspirational stories to tell of children's heightened response to correct guidance. Her professional pursuit paused when we had our own children, but while they were babies and toddlers, Rashmi used the very little spare time she had to learn more about little children, how they grow, what they need for healthy development, about what stimulates them, about what to do and what not to do. Every opportunity she got she visited reputed play schools in India and abroad and interacted with the children, the teachers and the principals. The idea that she could best serve her country by setting up a quality play school of her own grew in her heart and head. And in 1980, the idea manifested itself in the form of Toddlers Train, a nursery school she started with encouragement from her father-in-law, in the family home in Sunder Nagar in New Delhi.

Two decades later, in Toddlers Train's 20th Anniversary Commemorative Volume dated 18 February 2001, Rashmi wrote:

Completing two decades in the life of an institution, especially when this coincides with the beginning of a new millennium, is occasion enough to ponder a bit about the past and more so to think of the future... Toddlers Train began very modestly...(with) a small dream of my being purposefully engaged. Each year the School continued to grow and so did the dream of providing quality education to the very young. Today 20 years later, I feel blessed to have had the opportunity of serving so many children, of having been able to give good counsel to so many parents. It is so satisfying to meet the School's alumni and learn how well they are doing. It is so gratifying when some parents acknowledge that the inputs made at Toddlers Train constituted the solid foundation on which their children have grown so successfully.

The role that early childhood education plays in the development of a child has been known for long but is only just beginning to gain the recognition that it deserves. Toddlers Train's pragmatic approach to provide need based education to each child in a supportive environment that sensitizes the children to also recognize the needs of others and to be fair is clearly a good approach... Toddlers Train focuses on nurturing and empowering each and every child. It helps him/her to develop his/her self esteem and capabilities so that he/she grows up to be a caring and responsible citizen and a leader in today's competitive world.

Watching Toddlers Train grow, see so many children develop so beautifully and to observe Rashmi grow with them has been a very rare experience for me. Rashmi's constant desire, her will and her actions to make meaningful inputs to young children and her sadness at how our Nation is lacking in this respect, vis-à-vis such a huge population of young ones, have played on my mind all these years. Yes, it is important for a nation to have a good higher education system and institutes, it is necessary to have a good school system and education must be treated as the right of every child, but it is absolutely imperative to have a quality system to cater to our youngest from age 0 to 6. Besides this being a scientific fact, this is Rashmi's belief, her experience and her cure for the Nation.

Rashmi believes that we must view our youngest children as being the designers of the future and therefore we must endow them with worthy values and provide them with the fullest opportunities to blossom and flourish so that in due course they are able to create and construct with excellence. This has been Rashmi's life that I was so fortunate to have her share with me and Rashmi's glow slowly but surely penetrated into my brain. Rashmi and her belief are my inspiration for writing this Book to draw your attention to the youngest in our Nation and, of course, in the entire world.

P.S. The first few pages of a book usually also state to whom the book is *dedicated to*. This Book is not *dedicated to* anyone. Instead, as you may have inferred, and as will become amply evident as you read it, the Book is *directed at*.

'*Directed at*', you question.

Yes, *directed at*.

It is *directed at*:

the parents	who bring children into this world and then it is their responsibility to give them the best opportunity to blossom
the intelligentsia	who should have no difficulty in comprehending that the pre-school years are the most crucial and critical
the activists	who look to work for good causes – this is the best one
the media	who are constantly covering the 'breaking' – let them try promoting the 'building' for a change
the policy makers	who usually focus on the short-term – let them recognize for once that it is the long term that is really relevant

and it is *directed at* all of us

who want not just *achhe din* (good days) but an *achha yug* (good era).

P.P.S. In the 20th Anniversary Commemorative Volume, Rashmi also wrote: 'All these years, the School resisted the temptation to be drawn into engaging in any populist pursuit…' Children enrolled in Toddlers Train because parents of children in School advised their friends to admit their children to it. The School occasionally placed an advertisement in neigbourhood publications or to support some cause, but did not spend thousands on advertising campaigns. It flourished by word of mouth. This Book draws from experiences at Toddlers Train but it is not an advertising medium for Toddlers Train since, after the academic year 2016-2017, Toddlers Train will be wearing a different mantle.

Gimme Five

SOME of us, who have a Westernized orientation, often approach a child with a face that is glowing, a smile that is the broadest, eyes that are sparkling, a gait that has a lilt, and enticingly say or rather squeak, 'gimme five' … 'gimme five' … 'gimme five' and we are tickled no end if and when the child lifts his hand and gives our extended hand a tap with his hand.

'Gimme five' is an infectious invitation, and if one extends it to a toddler at a gathering or a picnic, all the adults line up before the kids demanding 'gimme five'. And, with each success the tempo rises higher and higher.

We surmise a great deal from the child's reciprocative gesture: the child is growing up; the child is beginning to respond; the child has accepted us as a friend. We are thrilled. We revel in ourselves. We hug the child. We show off to the other adults. The child has listened to us and replied in kind. Were the child able to articulate, he would also have probably said, 'gimme five'.

But what might be the 'five' that the child would really want? In this Book the focus is on children between the age of 0 to 6 - known the world over as the pre-school years.

The five needs that are described hereafter are every child's needs. Not just of a child born into a family with a Westernized orientation or one that is well off but also of the child of the have-nots. Surely we can appreciate that a child, any child anywhere in the world, beginning his journey on this earth is unaware of the socio-economic status of his parentage; its significance and implications dawn on the child only later, as the child begins to grow up.

To begin with, for the child, the world that the child has come into must seem a most weird, bewildering and unpredictable place. A place that is sometimes hot and sometimes cold, dry or wet, lit-up or dark, soundless or noisy. It must be confusing the child, frightening the child and only rarely amusing the child. The child must have a desperate need for *security* and for being wanted, protected and loved.

Second, a child's immune system is extremely delicate. Exposure to infection can quickly lead to disease and illness and even death. The death rate of children is directly proportional to the lack of cleanliness of the *environment* in which they grow up.

Next, the child experiences hunger. It must get the food appropriate for the child's age so that the child can grow with strong bones, healthy blood, and all the sensory and other organs functioning optimally. The child needs food that provides the best *nutrition*.

The greater the variety of activities a child is given the *opportunity* to engage in, the greater is the development of the child's capabilities and personality. A child that is ignored can get hurt and one who is rigidly controlled and not allowed new experiences will be stunted for life. This fourth need is to be given the opportunity to explore and experience.

Finally, the child needs sustained and good *guidance*. What is the appropriate time to move the child to his own bed to sleep on? When should one stop feeding the child, and the child be coaxed to eat on his own? How should the child be inducted into developing an interest in music? How should one respond to the child when he throws a tantrum? What empowers a child? What spoils a child? We, the adults, have to provide the right answers.

But are we? Are we satisfying these five needs of the child? Let us call them his *SENOG*: loving *S*ecurity, clean *E*nvironment, best *N*utrition, ample *O*pportunity, and good *G*uidance.

Legend has it that nature took care of the first need of the child: *security*. A mother is supposed to be naturally disposed to care for her child. There are numerous stories in folklore and elsewhere about the maternal instinct, and about how motherly love prompts a woman to invariably place the child's needs before and above her own. Stories about how she starves so that her child can have a bite; how she braves the cold to snuggle the child into warmth, and so on. These are not just stories, but reality.

Alas, they are not uniformly true. There are also ample stories now of how after childbirth, some mothers count the days to get back to their jobs, the buzz of their office and the social whirl in general, content to leave the infant in the care of the *ayah* (maid), or nanny, and in the not so opulent households, of the granny. Among the have-nots, the mother is forced to get back to earning the livelihood and the baby is attended to or ignored by elder siblings or the extended family.

If you cannot look after your child why give birth to one? The question is now not only being frequently asked but is being actually manifested in lower birth rates. In an article in *Forbes Asia Magazine* of May 2012, Lee Kuan Yew, the late founding father and first Prime Minister of Singapore, sounded a warning bell for his own country and many European countries where the birth rate is less than the 'replacement rate', i.e., the rate of reproduction that keeps a population stable. He stated, 'To have babies is, of course, a personal decision, but for a nation's population that decision carries considerable consequences. The education of our women and their ability to be high-income earners have altered social behavior and led to marriages later in life. But when women put off having children until their mid-30s, they have fewer children.' And sometimes none.

The second need of the child - to grow up in a clean *environment* - has both macro and micro aspects. Macro, that is, all about carbon emissions, global warming, atmospheric pollution, solid waste disposal, impure water, nuclear hazards and so on. International dialogue, discussion, negotiation, mediation and all that engages the top echelons of scientists and diplomats of developed, developing and under-developed countries and all this because of the undisputed, favourite catch phrase – 'We must leave the world safe for our children.' So be it. At the micro level, we worry about the cleanliness of our city, our streets, our neighbourhood and indeed that of the inside our own homes. Control over sewage and garbage disposal, having good drainage after heavy rainfall, prohibiting burning of leaves and other foliage, not celebrating with fire-crackers, shoeing away mosquitoes and flies and ensuring that the children wash their hands after that and before this. Those of us with reasonable economic resources and well-developed state of awareness of issues of hygiene are able to provide our children with a clean environment to grow up in. Unfortunately, there are millions and millions of children who are forced to live in an environment that is severely wanting. Urban slums and undeveloped rural habitats are homes to far too many children and many of them are unable to cope with it and prematurely leave this world. Every government of every country claims that it is working towards remedying this situation, and they *have* remedied it—but only to varying degrees. In our own country, one can only wonder why after years and years of governmental effort, so little has been achieved.

The story of the third need of children for the best *nutrition* is very similar to that of clean environment. The well-off have the wherewithal to satisfy these needs and most do so reasonably well. Amongst them are also the indulgent and not-so-knowledgeable parents who over-indulge the children with fast-food and junk-food, with dire consequences for them in adulthood. There are, however, an enormous number of the not so well-to-do who are unable to feed their children well.

Forget about nutritious food, they are not even able to provide sufficient food. Some private initiatives have attempted to address this issue, and they are to be commended, but given the magnitude of the problem they are just a drop in a very large bucket. One constantly hopes that a time will come when the numbers of the poverty-stricken will be negligible, if not zero.

The chief concern in this Book is with the fourth and fifth needs of the child below six years. How can we provide that child with ample *opportunity* and good *guidance* to grow to his maximum potential.

The Book is divided into three parts.

The first part describes the scientific discoveries that have been unearthed in relation to ensuring that the child develops to his maximum potential. Research by neurobiologists has generated a clear picture of how a brain develops. The specifics are not easy for everyone to comprehend but all of us can understand the basic mechanisms that have been identified, and even more, begin to appreciate the probable consequences of our doing this or not doing that when bringing up our children. Just to drive home the point of how important these first few years of a child are, John Watson, the founder of modern behaviourism claimed:

> 'Give me a dozen healthy infants, well-formed, and my own specified world to bring them up in and I'll guarantee to take any one at random and train him to become any kind of specialist I might select – doctor, lawyer, artist, merchant-

chief, and yes even beggar-man and thief, regardless of his talents, penchants, abilities, vocations, and race of his ancestors.'

(From John Watson's book on *"Behaviourism"* 1924
as quoted by L. Stevenson in his book
"Seven Theories of Human Nature", New York:
Oxford University Press, 1974, p. 93)

Clearly Watson was overstating the influence of nurture over nature but at the same time he was highlighting the importance of the early years of the life of a child when the brain is most malleable. Clearly then, the best way to ensure that our children grow up well is to provide them the opportunities they need and the guidance that encourages growth and development. These discoveries are so fantastic that they call for a major change in our national education policy and that change will never see the light of day unless many of us first understand the nature of these discoveries, then explain them to others, and, as seems to be the pattern these days, then broadcast them, then take out processions on the streets and sit on *dharnas* (non-violent sit-in protests). So let us make the beginning.

The second part of the Book discusses the many ways in which children are being brought up in different parts of the world and what the various governments are doing for their pre-school children. Not only are there quantitative as well as qualitative issues that are relevant, but each country has its unique socio-economic scenario that impinges on policy-formulation and implementation. For example, Japan is so concerned about its declining birth-rate and the changing values of motherhood, as well as the role of women in society, that these dominate the government's decision-making on issues relating to pre-school children.

The third part describes the situation in our own country. Our children of age 0 to 6 have found mention in our Constitution in 2002, five-and-a-half decades after Independence, through amended Article 45 (The Constitution Act, 2002) which directs that '*The State shall endeavour to provide ECCE for all children until they complete the age of six years*'. And this is only a directive principle and not a right for our young children to receive Early Childhood Care and Education (ECCE). The Right of Children to Free and Compulsory Education Act, 2009, takes effect only when they attain the age of 6 and up to the age of 14, that is, from class 1 to class 8. As far as the pre-school children of age 0–6 years are concerned, this Act in its Section 11 merely states: '*With a view to prepare children above the age of three years for elementary education and to provide ECCE for all children until they complete the age of six years, the appropriate government may make necessary arrangement for providing free pre-primary education for such children.*' So, the 'appropriate' government 'may', and then again, it 'may not'.

These three parts of the Book are interspersed with short delectable anecdotes of how some very typical child-centered situations were or can be effectively resolved, as well as some interesting stories, thoughts and tidbits, mostly from my wife's play school.

The Book concludes with a plea to our national policy-makers to take a fresh look at the education policy and revise it to focus on empowerment of the child at the child's most crucial age – the pre-school age from years 0 to 6, and not cling on to unscientific methods and belittling reservation policies for grown-ups who were underprivileged and neglected in their childhood.

'GIMME FIVE' says the child! So, let us respond by assuming the responsibility we tacitly chose to undertake when we brought our children into this world, and provide them the SENOG they need!

PART I

THE SCIENTIFIC REALM

Brainputer

WHEN electronic computers impinged on our consciousness in the middle of the last century, people would describe them as machines with electronic brains that worked logically. By the end of that century, computers were very much part of our daily lives, as we grew to rely on them to seek and store information, to process data, to communicate with each other and for a myriad other functions. For many it became a permanent add-on to oneself. They carried it with them where ever they went. They could not do without it. And to facilitate that, the gadget was modified and reinvented and it became smaller and smaller and smaller.

In five or so decades, the computer became such a familiar device that instead of explaining it as an electronic brain, one began to use the computer to explain the nature of the human brain. Neurobioligist Lise Eliot in her book *What's Going On In There? How the Brain and Mind Develop in the First Five Years of Life*, draws upon our familiarity with the computer to explain how a child's brain develops and functions. This explanation is far easier to comprehend than the explanation she presents in neurobiological terms, as will shortly become evident.

Let us begin first in neurobiological lingo. As per Lise Eliot, the formation of the brain begins as early as nineteen days after fertilization at a time when parents may not be even aware of the fact that the mother has conceived. The beginning is through the formation of the tiniest brain tissue which starts off the process of neurulation. The process moves rapidly: the bottom of a neural tube moves on to become the spinal cord; from the tube's top emerge the forebrain, the midbrain and the hindbrain. By six weeks, the fore, the mid and the hindbrain take the form of seven parts of the brain: pons, medulla, cerebellum, thalamus, basal ganglia, limbic system and cerebral cortex.

First to develop in the brain are those structures that control a human's basic functions, such as breathing and feeding. The more intellectual functions of the brain, like the capacity to communicate and to reason, come later.

The development of brain, explains Lise Eliot, is a threefold process of neurogenesis, synaptogenisis and myelination. Neurogenesis consists of the formation and growth of neurons. A neuron is like a tree with an elaborate root system known as the dendrites, a trunk known as the axon, and branches that are designated as presynaptic terminals. Dendrites receive input from other neurons, the axon transmits it to the presynaptic terminals and they in turn pass it on to the dendrite of another neuron in the circuit. Neurons are produced at an enormous rate, to the order of half a million neurons per minute in the first four-and-a-half months of gestation, adding up to 100 billion of them. Many circuits need to be formed in the brain for the brain to do all it has to. For a circuit to form as required, the presynaptic terminal of one neuron has to connect with the dendrite of another appropriate neuron. Making this connection is known as synapse formation or synaptogenisis. This is followed by myelination and that ensures that the connection is firm and protected rather like covering the connection of two electric wires with insulation tape.

The 100 billion neurons produced during the first half of the gestation period, also during this period, migrate to the final position they are destined to take in the brain. Each neuron is also busy in generating its dendrites and continues to do so even after birth. Imagewise, the brain is akin to a very, very dense forest of neurons each with its roots, trunk and branches that keep becoming bigger and more complex with time.

For the brain to function, the process of synapse formation is crucial, highlights Lise Eliot, since it is the point that ensures communication between two neurons. Synapse formation also occurs at a tremendous rate; during the last two months of gestation and for two years after birth, synapses in a part of the brain are formed at the rate of 1.8 million synapses per second. How does one neuron know which other neuron it needs to have a synapse connection with? It is only on account of having the correct connections that what the ears hear, the brain receives, comprehends, interprets, and then through other connections instructs the vocal cords to respond in a particular manner. Or if the finger touches something hot, the correct connection of neurons pass this stimulus to the brain which then sends the message back to the finger to snatch itself away from the hot object and all this happens in an instant. Clearly, nature is able to craft itself so that the correct connections are formed to make the necessary circuits.

Whether a child is born in the luxury of an opulent home or without a roof over his head, it takes about the same amount of time, plus or minus a few days or at most a few weeks, for each child to be able to sit, or to crawl, or to walk and so on. In addition to nature, a child is also born with genes from the parents and these genes assist in synapse formation so that the child is enriched with an inheritance unique to each child.

In early childhood, beginning from infancy the synapses that are produced by the cerebral cortex are about two times the synapses that the system will eventually require. What is produced is rather diffused and that is what results in a system that is not very clear or precise in terms of transferring information. Apparently this is so because nature and genes can only go so far in outfitting a child for life. The fine-tuning is left to the nurturing that a child is provided with, and this is where the environment of the child, the care the child receives, the training that is provided, take over. Synapses that are called into action get stabilized and those that are lying dormant because of lack of stimuli and use whither away and perish and are lost forever. This is why it is said that the child's brain is most malleable in the first 5 to 6 years of the child's life. If during this period, the child is exposed to all varieties of play, all varieties of sounds, all varieties of experiences, in short all varieties of stimuli, the child's brain grows and the child becomes capable of competently handling all that the child has been exposed to.

Be it the familiarity with multiple languages, with numbers and mathematics, or being explorative or being skilful in playing games, musical instruments, sketching and painting, making things with ones hands and so on. On the other hand, if the child is not provided with sufficient stimuli in some spheres, the child loses the relevant synapses in those spheres forever. Many of us have experienced how quickly a child learns a number of languages if the child is in an environment where more than one language is in use, whereas, later as an adult, attempting to learn a new language is such a pain. It is a pain since the facility of making new synapses has diminished to a trickle.

One cannot overemphasize how important the early years are in the growth and development of the child's brain, and therefore the child's capacities and personality. According to Howard Gardner, Professor in Cognition and Education at Harvard Graduate School of Education

> '...Gusii mothers in southwestern Kenya hold their infants three times as much as do American mothers, while American middle-class mothers spend far more time talking to and looking at their infants...such strongly contrasting cultural practices and expectations accumulate over time to yield children and adults who are characteristic of their own culture.'

(From Howard Gardner, "*The Unschooled Mind – How Children Think and How Schools Should Teach*" published by Basic Books, Tenth-Anniversary Edition, 2004, p. 53)

Upon growing up, this results in Gussi children being comfortable in a familiar family environment and behaving with due respect to their elders, whereas, American children are more extrovert in their behaviour and more free in expressing themselves and pursuing their interests. This is why the behaviour of children brought up in one culture often appears quite awkward when they are amongst those of different culture. The neurons with their dendrites, axons and presynaptic terminals, are there in much more than ample abundance in every child's growing brain – it is the synapses that are allowed to be formed with repeated stimuli that survive, whereas the synapses that are not nurtured are the ones that are lost and vanish for ever.

The Times of India of 27 December 2012 carried a story with the headline, 'Net overuse leaving kids brain-dead'. *Oops*, I reacted, is this a terrorist attack by the machines designed to enslave human beings by killing our brains? The story presented the views of a leading British inventor, Trevor Baylis, who had invented the wind-up radio and then, at the age of 75, was appalled because children spent too much time in front of screens. He stated, 'Children have got to be taught hands-on and not to become mobile phone or computer dependent… children will become fairly brain-dead if they become so dependent on the Internet.' He was worried 'that the next generation of inventors is being lost, with young people often unable to make anything with their hands.' He lauded toys like Meccano and 'the old-fashioned way'. You may not have heard of Trevor Baylis and may discount his views given that he was 75 when he wrote that, growing old and not 'with it', but everyone has heard of Steve Jobs, the Apple founder; according to a story in the *International New York Times* of 10 September 2014 by Nick Bilton, he writes that during a conversation he had with Steve Jobs in late 2010, when Jobs was asked how his children liked the iPad, Jobs replied: 'They haven't used it. We limit how much technology our kids use at home.' Subsequently, Bilton reached out to Steven Job's biographer Walter Issacson who spent a lot of time at their home. 'Every evening,' Issacson told him, 'Steve made a point of having dinner at the big long table in their kitchen, discussing books and history and a variety of things,' he said. 'No one ever pulled out an iPad or computer. The kids did not seem addicted at all to devices.'

I also recall the advantages of the old-fashioned way. When I was kid and when my mom used to bathe me, it was time for me to recite the multiplication tables and answer questions she posed to hone my ability in oral arithmetic. Three decades ago, I was shopping in a store in the U.S., carefully converting the price of each item into Rs. then weighing the price of each item vis-à-vis its utility. When I finished shopping, I rounded off the price of each of the six items I had selected to buy and in my head added up the six figures to total approximately $47. I took out $50 from my wallet and went to the cashier. She punched in the cost of the six items on her cash register and demanded $59.35. I told her that her figure was wrong and that it should be about $47. She looked at me aghast, and said, 'This is what it says here and this is electronic.' I insisted that something was wrong. She insisted it wasn't. The queue behind me was becoming longer. The folks right behind me sniggered at this brown chap questioning the figure on the cash register. The girl behind the counter was getting exasperated. I suggested she punch in the figures again. Most reluctantly she agreed and then her eyes opened wide with surprise and, mustering up lots of courage, she muttered, 'It now says $46.95'. I replied, 'That sounds better.' The folks right behind me heard all this and began whispering to those behind them and the whispering continued down the line. Meanwhile, I handed over $50, collected my change of $3 and a nickel and took off thinking of my childhood baths and feeling grateful to my mom.

The Times of India, of two days later, that is, of 29 December 2012, published another story from London with the headline 'Babysitter gadgets up speech problem in kids – 1.2 m in UK face communication difficulties'. A government-funded study had revealed that 'as many as 1.2 million young Britons struggle with speech… the rise is being blamed on the growing use of screen-based gadgets as convenient "babysitters", a trend for hard-working parents to spend less time with their children.' Jean Gross, a former government speech and language expert, bemoans the use of screen-based technology such as TVs, games consoles, smartphones and computers in lieu of traditional family activities such as learning nursery rhymes and reciting them together.

All will agree that the new computer-based technology is great; it plays many useful roles and enables us to do things that we never dreamt were possible. Problems arise when it begins to dominate the lives of children. If the child is not being engaged in multiple activities and the child is not receiving a variety of stimuli, some synapses will never form and to that extent the child will be handicapped. Be it the handicap of not being able to use one's hands to make things and eventually come up with inventions, as is the concern of Trevor Baylis – or the handicap of the most basic form: the ability to speak, to form words and sentences and communicate, because the synapses that enable the child to do so have not been formed since the child did not receive sufficient stimuli in that realm.

In view of the current general familiarity with the computer, this is perhaps an opportune time to present the nature of the human brain in computer terminology. Lise Eliot writes,

> 'Imagine that you bought a PC, but instead of loading any software, you just plugged it in and the computer did the rest: it assembled its own operating system, and built its own drivers for the CD-ROM'
>
> (From Lise Eliot, *What's Going on in There – How the Brain and Mind Develop in the First Five Years of Life,* published by Bantam Books 1999 and herein the 2000 paperback edition p. 8 and 9)

and, also for all the other hardware that it has equipment for, say the printer, the sound system, the modem etc. As the PC begins to function and it needs a word-processing programme it makes one; when it needs to calculate, it sets up a spreadsheet programme and so on. In other words, consider the child's brain to be a computer, a 'brainputer' that also has the capacity to programme itself. Lise Eliot continues,

> 'Children's brains are like this, accessing neural-circuits as they are needed, wiring them up and honing them to the task at hand'
>
> (Ibid., p. 9)

whether it be to stand up, to walk, to climb, to talk, to sing, to play with blocks, etc. This PC you have bought builds itself up only if you place demands on it, and builds itself up only *for* the demands you place on it. So also, the child's brain, if during the time window provided, that is early childhood, no demands are placed on it, let us say, that are music-related, then the wiring provided for playing the piano, appreciating the melody, recognizing the beat, decays and rots and is lost. Building the same capacity in later years is not impossible but far more tedious and rarely ever of the quality that would have been possible if appropriate stimuli had reached the neurons to make synapses during early childhood.

What Stimuli, When, How, by Whom?

SO children need stimuli to enable their brains to develop. Are parents and care-givers expected to provide the stimuli? Do children provide the stimuli themselves? What kinds of stimuli should these be? When are the children most receptive to different kinds of stimuli? Plenty of questions! So, let us begin at the beginning.

When a newly married couple takes the good news to their respective parents that they will soon become grandparents, the latter are thrilled – usually much more than the couple themselves. The couple's joy is tempered with thoughts of new responsibilities; the grandparents are busy conjuring up visions of delectable playmates. Then their thoughts go back to the time when they were expecting their first child and all that they had experienced in those fateful nine months. They immediately become serious and the advice pours forth: 'Make sure that the next nine months are stress-free for the mom-to-be'; 'She must eat good nutritious food'; 'No smoking'; 'No drinking'; 'Regular light exercise'; 'Go for a walk morning and evening'; 'Focus on good thoughts'; 'Read good books'; 'Listen to good music' and so on. Clearly, the thinking is that as the baby's brain is being formed in the mom-to-be's womb, it is susceptible to being influenced by everything that the mom-to-be does and experiences during this period.

This may once have been folklore but it is no more just that, its worth is being substantiated by scientific research. The baby's developing brain is not just vulnerable to the bad but also burgeons with the good. As an example of the bad, according to Lise Eliot, when a mom-to-be, during pregnancy is overstressed, her hormone levels reach high levels and the fetus may get an overdose of corticosteroids and catecholamines which interfere with brain function and can lead to a baby who is more fussy and irritable and the baby's development, both mental and motor can also get delayed.

And, as an example of the good, Lise Eliot endorses the idea that the fetus responds positively to mom-to-be's moderate exercise since exercise makes the mom-to-be feel good and the fetus's heart rate also increases. The response to strenuous exercise is, however, not good as revealed by measurement of fetal heart rate which apparently begins to drop. The best exercise is swimming and jogging in the pool since water helps to dissipate the heat that develops in mom-to-be's body. And, after nine long months that seemed much longer than nine, because of being constantly careful, the baby arrives.

Nature does not send the baby unequipped into the world. Nature also has the mother sensitized to care for her baby.

When the mother picks up her new-born baby, she naturally cuddles the baby, naturally hugs the baby, naturally squeezes the baby next to her chest and breasts, naturally kisses the baby on the face on the arms on almost every part of the body, naturally strokes the baby gently and lovingly – the baby's skin feels the mother's skin – through these actions all generating a touch sensation, love travels from the mom to the baby and the baby's brain grows as it registers the sensation – the baby revels in it. A bond is established.

Thereafter, whenever the baby experiences discomfort, it pines for the mom's cuddle and the mom is instantly there for the baby. Can one imagine how distressed a baby would be if it did not receive the mom's cuddle? The touch sensation is clearly the first stimulation that the baby needs, comprehends, and through it the baby's brain develops. Nature has the mother and the baby conditioned to provide and receive these stimuli. The mother doesn't need to read books and listen to lectures and be trained to develop these skills. Nature has taken care of them.

Move from nature to nurture, and cuddling transforms to carefully orchestrated full-body massage for the baby. Infant massage is a well-established tradition in our country. A massage helps the blood circulation and body growth. This touch therapy impacts not just the body but also the brain. Many studies have now shown that a daily massage is great for children's well-being – it lowers their stress levels and anxiety, improves their pattern of sleep and enhances their level of responsiveness.

Of the five senses, touch is clearly the one that a newborn child responds to first. Smell and taste follow soon thereafter, triggered by the child's recognition of his mom's natural odour and the delicious taste of the milk from her breasts. Breast milk is well known to be the best food for the child. Not only does it have all the right nutrients, minerals and vitamins, it also has factors that enhance immunity, and the necessary hormones and enzymes. Formula milk provides the mother with some convenience but as far as the child is concerned, it is just no match for the real thing.

Our expert biotechnologists have not yet succeeded in replicating all the goodness of breast milk. Apparently, the ingestion of breast milk impacts on the brain as well, since research is leading scientists to conclude that mental development of children who are breast-fed, in comparison to those who are bottle-fed is superior: not only do they perform better in intelligence tests conducted during preschool period but also do better in scholastic achievement tests during school years up to age ten. What's more, the longer babies are breast-fed the higher is their IQ. Diligent mothers pay scant heed to the inconvenience they themselves suffer and stick to their resolve to breast-feed the baby for the entire first year.

Hearing, the fourth sense, does not lag too far behind as the child begins to respond to those lovely lullabies, a stimulus that lulls the brain and relaxes the child and then ever so gently the child drifts into sleep. Sight is the sense that is the last to get going. Upon birth, when the child's eyes are open, they only see a kind of blur, and it takes about six months before they can focus with their eyes. This becomes so apparent when one observes the child's eyes following the moving sound of two clicking fingers as a dad moves his hand left to right and then back to left above the face of his lovely child as the child lies on his lap. Six months more, at the age one year, the baby's vision is similar to an adult's.

And, once all the five sensory faculties are activated, the fun begins. The child begins to explore. Give the child any object and he will look at it and feel it. If the object does not make a sound, the child will shake it to see if it does. And before you know it, the child will move the object to his mouth to taste it and then in order to complete the inspection, smell it. If the object does not excite any interest, that is it does not tickle the brain in any manner, the child will dump it and look for another object.

The exploration begins in earnest once the child can crawl. The child no longer needs to have objects brought to him; he will crawl to whatever interests him and is within crawling reach. The new discovered mobility and the consequent feeling of independence give the child an enormous high. You have heard grown-ups advise that you let the child crawl wherever he safely can, and that the more he crawls, the more intelligent he will become. In other words, exploration helps the brain to grow, 'just like travel broadens the mind'! Exploration through crawling is perhaps safer than when the child is standing up and walking. The child through crawling can reach only a few objects, and supervising adults do not have to say, 'No, don't touch that!' quite so often. According to John Holt, a great proponent of the home-schooling movement, children are not at all pleased to hear us restricting them with 'no no'. Whenever they hear the 'no no', they feel they are being attacked and not being allowed to explore what surrounds them and become familiar with all of it.

> 'Everyone else touches this; why can't I? It is easy to see how too much of such treatment would destroy a child's curiosity, and make him or her feel that the world, instead of being full of interesting things to explore and think about, is full of hidden dangers and ways of getting into trouble.'
>
> (From John Holt, *How Children Learn*, published by Penguin Books, Revised Edition 1983, p. 31)

In effect, we are curbing a very desirable trait in the child to explore and learn and not allowing the brain to grow. Before the child becomes mobile it is our job to child-proof the house, so that the we don't have to say 'no' too often. And, as the child learns and his brain develops, one can gradually begin to bring back all that we had put away during child-proofing and let the child learn about the more fragile, the possibly dangerous, objects that also have a place in the house.

Children not only like to explore but like to do so on their own or as per Holt, they do not even like being given help when they have not asked for it. It is difficult for us to comprehend how intelligent little children can be and how capable. And unlike what the 'sane' advise us, little children are far more skillful and resourceful than they get credit for. They develop these capabilities if we encourage them to develop them and exploring is what provides them the stimuli needed for synapses to form in the brain and the brain to grow. If we over control children to cater to our fears, we end up just retarding their growth and the opportunity for many synapses to form is lost forever.

Given the opportunity, children begin to develop many skills. Pouring water from one glass into another without spilling it, arranging blocks one on top of another, matching the shape of a hole and that of the object seeking to enter it so that they can drop the object through the correct hole, picking up food in a spoon and transporting it and putting it into their mouth, beating a stick on a drum at a steady pace, and many, many other things. They learn by seeing the grown-ups do these things and then by imitating the adults. Again, children do not need and do not appreciate too much adult help as they attempt, fail, attempt again, partially succeed, and then gradually perfect doing something. Not only are they learning skills, they are also learning to feel a variety of emotions of which perhaps self-esteem is the most important one. Adults must very consciously behave in a manner that enhances the child's opinion of himself. That is what keeps the child going from one skill to the next more difficult one, and then even more complex ones.

As the child grows, the environment of the home is not enough. There is so much to explore beyond. There is the sky above and the earth below. There are streets that lead to parks, maybe to the waterfront, to the base of a mountain or the edge of a cliff. There are birds that fly by, dogs that bark, cats that mew and who knows maybe even a cow and more. The most exciting thing is of course that there are other children – some a little older, some younger – who are out also on a mission to explore and get to know the world they inhabit.

There are experts who know how to help the child to develop. Among the many experts who have focused on how to help children and their brains to grow, one who has had an enormous impact was Maria Montessori (1870–1952). An Italian by birth, she became the first woman to qualify in Italy as a medical doctor. She became interested in the needs of children and devoted her life to devise methods suitable for the development of children. Her success led to international recognition and for over four decades, she travelled all over the world training and promoting schools, even in prisons where infants were held captive along with their errant mothers, that adopted her methodology. Her basic approach was to recognize that:

1. Every child was born with the potential for creativity, a desire to learn and the right to be accepted as an individual.
2. Each child needed an environment both at home and at school that was conducive to his development - an environment that provided the child with freedom to experience and experiment.

3. Children needed specially designed learning materials which would, through sensory stimulation, help them explore and then, as their brain developed, comprehend.
4. And finally, that each child needed to be provided the opportunity to develop at his own unique pace.

The Abecedarian Project and More

THAT a child's brain is most malleable during his early days, weeks, months and years is a strong reason for us, the adults, to make the necessary inputs in this crucial period so that the child develops to his full potential. The significance of this has been amazingly highlighted by a project initiated in the early 1970s at the FPG Child Development Institute of the University of North Carolina (FPG CDI UNC) in the United States known as the Abecedarian Project.

For this project, the University persuaded individuals of low-income families, most of them of African-American origin, to permit it to study the development of 111 children born to these families between 1972 to 1977. The 111 infants between the ages of 6 to 12 weeks were randomly placed in two groups. Of these, 57 infants constituted Group-A. They were provided carefully designed child-care that included high-quality educational inputs from infancy to age 5 years. The remaining 54 infants, Group-B, received child-care at home or other places as per the wishes of their parents. Each of these two groups were later split further into two sub-groups. For some children of Group-A, let us say children of Group-A1, the provision of quality inputs ceased at age 5, whereas for the rest of the children of the group, that is, Group-A2, the quality inputs continued until age 8. For the children of Group-B1, the pattern followed up to age 5 continued thereafter, whereas for the rest of the children of the group, Group-B2, quality inputs were provided beginning at age 5 and up to age 8 years.

From infancy to age 5, children in Group A attended the programme that started at 7:30 am and concluded at 5:30 pm daily for 50 weeks in the year. The children were provided free transport. The teacher-to-child ratio was maintained at 1 to 3 for infants and toddlers and from 1 to 6 for older children. Children were treated to a game-based programme that encouraged intensive back-and-forth interaction between the children and the teachers. Teachers were provided with a large set of games and they were encouraged to customize the use of the games for each child as per the child's desire, need and stage of development. The games focused substantially on language development but also on motor-skills and activities designed for social and emotional development.

Assessments of the 111 children were conducted when they were aged 5 years, 8 years, then 12 and then 15 years. As many as 104 of the 111 were successfully contacted for assessment even when they had reached the age of 21 years.

To begin with, comparison of children in Group-A1 and Group-A2 indicated that the early childhood intervention (age

0-5) exerted a more powerful effect on the child's intelligence and academic outcomes than did the extra later intervention (5-8 years). Thus the focus of follow-up studies as the children grew in age was on comparing children in Group A with those of Group B.

Assessments up to 15 years of age indicated significant positive effects of early intervention as determined from achievement tests in mathematics and in reading as well as in intelligence. In addition, there were much fewer cases of children having to repeat an academic year or needing placement in special education classes.

At the age of 21, the positive effects of early interventions observed included, 'enhanced academic achievement, a greater likelihood of going to college, a reduction in teenaged parenthood, greater likelihood of obtaining skilled employment as a young adult, a trend for reduced smoking, and reduced use of marijuana' (as per the Policy Brief entitled 'Poverty and Early Childhood Educational Intervention' by Elizabeth P. Pungello and Frances A. Campbell of FPG of UNC, and W. Steven Barnett of National Institute for Early Education Research, Rutgers University, 2006). In quantitative terms: 36per cent of Group A attended college compared to 14 per cent of Group B; 47 per cent of Group A were in skilled employment compared to 27 per cent of Group B; 26 per cent of Group A became teen-parents compared to 45 per cent of Group B; 39 per cent of Group A smoked tobacco compared to 55 per cent of Group B and 18 per cent of Group A used marijuana compared to 39 per cent of Group B.

Clearly, from the Abecedarian Project one can deduce two very important observations:

1. The effect of quality and appropriate interventions made from age 0 to 5 years are far more significant than those made from the age 5 to 8 years.
2. Quality and appropriate interventions made from age 0 to 5 have a lasting effect well into the adult years.

Pungello, Campbell and Barnett conclude, 'Clearly, the effects of these early experiences can be long-lasting. Beyond providing a safe care setting, early care environments should provide cognitive stimulation as well. This stimulation need not consist of bringing down a kindergarten curriculum, but rather the provision of age-appropriate learning opportunities. To that end, society needs to recognize the importance of dedicating resources to the early years, before children reach formal schooling and enter kindergarten. Resources are needed to increase the quality of care available (such as through teacher training and education and the provision of age-appropriate materials) as well as to increase the access to the high quality settings for disadvantaged families through subsidies and other economic mechanisms. Learning begins in infancy, and many poor families must rely on external child care for their infants. The opportunity for enhancing the early development of these children must not be lost.'

HighScope Perry Preschool Study

A decade before the Abecedarian Project got started, the late David P. Weikart, founder of the HighScope Educational Research Foundation, an independent non-profit organization that has its headquarters in Ypsilanti, Michigan in the United States, initiated the HighScope Perry Preschool study and followed it through four decades. The study began in 1962, identifying 123 young African American children living in poverty in Ypsilanti. These children were unlikely to complete their school education and would have dropped out at various stages. The study randomly assigned 58 of the children to a high-quality 2-year early care and education programme at ages 3 and 4; the rest received no preschool programme. The programme offered to the 58 children consisted of two-and–a-half hours of classes on weekday mornings and one home visit to each mother and child for one-and-a-half hours once a week from October through May. Each teacher tended to only 5 to 6 children. The teachers engaged children in play activities and simultaneously encouraged them to make choices and solve problems, socially interact with other children and focused on developing the children both physically and intellectually.

Even though the Perry programme was not as intensive as the Abecedarian experiment, it yielded results that reinforce those of the Abecedarian study. In 2005, 97 per cent of the participants of the Perry programme, at the age of 40, were interviewed and data obtained about them from schools, social services and the police revealed that those who had gone through the preschool programme were doing better than those who had not. More had graduated from school, more were employed, they had made more money, more owned houses and cars and had savings accounts and the men of this group were more involved in raising their children and, perhaps most important, they had had fewer problems with the law and significantly fewer arrests.

Other Studies

Lest the skeptics amongst us discount the value of the two studies described above because both were conducted in America using African American children as subjects and that therefore they cannot and ought not to be used to make generalizations that would be applicable the world over, we only have to refer to the article entitled 'Early Childhood Programs in Other Nations: Goals and Outcomes' authored by Sarane Spence Boocock, Professor of Sociology at the Graduate School of Education at Rutgers University, and published in The Future of Children: Long-Term Outcomes of Early Childhood Programs Vol. 5, No. 3 – Winter 1995. The article describes and summarizes the results of 15 studies conducted in 13 countries: Australia, Canada, Colombia, France, Germany, India, Ireland, Japan, Singapore, South Korea, Sweden, Turkey, and the United Kingdom. These studies amply corroborate the findings of the Abecedarian and Perry programmes even though these studies were designed differently, each with its own methodology. Perhaps the single most important conclusion from these studies is that participating in a pre-school programme enables the child to perform better in school with less chances of failing and having to repeat a year.

From these 15 studies many other deductions have been made. Two of them are of particular relevance to our children who call out to us with 'Gimme Five'. First, children of low-income groups who are provided the opportunity to attend pre-school progrmmes gain more from them than those belonging to more advantaged groups. Obviously, the inputs that the latter receive from parental care and a more stimulating living environment help the child's brain to develop better, and the inputs from pre-school programmes provide only marginal benefit. And, this deduction has to be tempered by the second one, which highlights that the benefits that pre-school programmes generate tend to be commensurate with the quality and the emphasis of inputs. Poor-quality programmes (that exist only in name) yield very little benefit. But progammes focusing on cognitive issues help to ensure greater readiness for entering and performing better in regular schools. Programmes with inputs designed to increase the child's sociability, and encourage sharing and cooperating, showed positive results in that sphere.

The child's brain is highly malleable in the pre-school age. The richer the experience the child is provided during this age, the better the child's brain develops. It is up to us the adults and, for that matter, to a nation's policy-makers to design the inputs consistent with how we wish our children to be and behave when they grow up to be adults and citizens.

DELECTABLES I

Habits form Easily

GOOD or bad, habits form easily when one is three years of age or younger. In fact, they form very easily. And, once a habit has taken root, it lasts and lasts and lasts—unless one consciously and with concerted effort chooses to change it. But it is for us adults to choose the habits we wish to inculcate in our young ones.

Children's classrooms at Toddlers Train open onto a large verandah and from the verandah one takes a small step down onto the lawn in the front where the children come out to play during their allocated period.

Every day, children of each class, in turn, emerge out of their classroom with great excitement to enjoy their play time: they swing, they slide, they seesaw, they go round and round on the merry-go-round, and test themselves negotiating the horizontal and vertical rods of the jungle-gym, as well as have fun playing other games.

So that they do not carry any dirt or grime from the lawn onto the verandah and the classroom when they finish their play, they are advised to not just step up onto the verandah but take a prescribed route from the side of the verandah where there is a floor mat placed at the lawn level on which they wipe their shoes before stepping up to the verandah. A new child who joins the School, learns this quickly because the child is shown that if he doesn't the verandah gets dirty, because for a few days the child is reminded about this, because the child sees other children following the prescribed route up to the verandah – not just the other children but all the staff and teachers follow the same route and become the child's role models.

After each play period all the children head to the side of the verandah. There they queue up. Each, awaiting his/her turn and allowing everyone ahead in the queue, sufficient time to wipe the shoes before stepping up. There is no trying to jump the queue, no pushing, no shoving, no one falls down. Everyone and everything proceeds in an orderly manner.

This practice of wiping ones shoes before climbing onto the verandah is not followed only after play time but at all times: when they come in the morning to School, when they come after going to the bathroom and so on. And the practice doubles in value because it shows respect for those that cleaned the verandah and classes every morning before the children arrived and calls for no great effort or sacrifice and no great extra time. It is just a good habit, a worthy one to cultivate.

Children in School are taught many good habits. To throw litter only in the baskets provided. To place the toys they were playing with back on the rack after they finish with playing. To share their toys with other children. To finish all the food they brought as their tiffin and not waste any. And, so on. They learn quickly because this is the age when they are quick to put two and two together. If these good habits are not inculcated at this age, it becomes much more difficult, sometimes impossible, to cultivate them later on in adulthood.

Just imagine how 'world class' our cities would be if people did not litter them, did not spit on the streets, waited their turn in polite queues, did not dump food, did not honk all the time, let the car that has the right of way pass first, drove in our own lane, put the garbage in the correct bin, did not pee on trees and walls, nor mar them with posters, crossed the street at the zebra-crossing only when the signal indicated it was okay to do so—just imagine!

All these good habits are best inculcated in the youngest of our citizens. We, adults need to be the role models and those of us that are not will be ridiculed into learning good habits by the young citizens if we facilitate our young citizens to acquire these good habits when they are young.

Bindiya Won't Budge

MY wife Rashmi, Director of Toddlers Train, regularly shares with me interesting happenings in school: stories about, for instance, the behaviour of a child that was so cute and childlike and how it amused everyone. I relish them and laugh with pleasure. Sometimes, the account will be of some child who behaved so maturely that it amazed everyone and I pause to wonder at it. But most interesting are anecdotes that highlight how a child's potentially problematic behaviour was identified and tackled. These I found the most educative as did the parents of the concerned child. Here is one such anecdote as narrated by Rashmi:

'I heard some strange sounds emanating from the classroom as I was walking past its shut door. I decided to peep in. All the focus was on Bindiya, a very sweet little three-year-old girl. The teacher was standing at the side of the chair Bindiya was seated on, and Viraj, Bindiya's classmate, was standing beside the teacher.

'The teacher explained that for some days now Bindiya had chosen to sit on the particular chair she was then sitting on. Today, after returning from the play period outside, Viraj sat down on that chair. Bindiya, on coming into the classroom, wanted her seat back and Viraj told her to go sit elsewhere. Whereupon Bindiya kicked up a big fuss and Viraj finally had to get up and vacate the chair for her. The teacher was trying to talk Bindiya out of her insistence on sitting on *that* particular chair and *no other* chair but Bindiya was hanging on to it and refusing to budge.

'I totally agreed with the teacher remonstrating with her. Fixation of any kind at that young age was not to be encouraged. I told the teacher to let me try a different approach to achieve the desired end.

'I called out to the class, "Let us play a game!" and they all looked up expectantly. I told everyone to line up along one wall of the room. They did and that included Bindiya. I continued, "I am going to point to a chair, close my eyes and call out the name of one child and that child is to quickly go to that chair and sit on it before I open my eyes. If the child is not sitting on the chair when I open my eyes then he or she loses the game." I proceeded with my plan. I pointed to a chair, closed my eyes, called out a name and immediately there were hurried footsteps. When the footstep sounds ceased, I opened my eyes and clapped and invited all the children to clap for the child who had gone to the right chair and sat down. We proceeded: child after child after child and claps after claps after claps. During the course of the "game", Bindiya's name was also called and she enthusiastically went and sat on the pointed out chair that, by design, was not the chair she had a fixation for and we all clapped for her as well. After the game was over, I congratulated everyone, told them that they were all winners and walked out.

'After, School was over for the day, the teacher and I discussed the issue and I told her that tomorrow Bindiya would again grab her old seat. And that on some pretext or the other, the teacher should have her get up and use the opportunity to have her sit elsewhere.

'The next day, after School, Bindiya's teacher reported that sure enough, Bindiya came and sat on her old seat. The teacher asked her to go and pick up a toy from the rack and bring it to her. When Bindiya brought the toy, the teacher had her sit on a different chair and showed her how to play with that toy.

'This process went on for some days and Bindiya's teacher reported that she was improving. One day, I again walked into the class before the teacher had had a chance to move Bindiya out of her favourite spot. The moment Bindiya saw me enter, all on her own, she quietly slid into the seat next to her favourite one which happened to be unoccupied.

'After school, I told Bindiya's teacher that we had licked Bindiya's fixation problem and Bindiya's subsequent behaviour indicated that we indeed had.'

Every Child is a Winner

CHILDREN love to be in a garden, in fresh air, under the blue sky. They love to watch the birds flitting from one tree to the next and hear the squeaky, chirpy sounds they make. They are intrigued by the variety in the colours, shapes and scents of different flowers. They love to trace their little fingers around leaves—some so soft and some interestingly pokey. They love to put everything in their mouth and check if something is tasty. They just love the splendour of choices that nature offers their senses.

They love to walk, hop, jump, run forward and sideways and back. They love to kneel, to squat, to lie down. One moment they are down inspecting the little insect they saw moving up a blade of grass and the next moment they are reaching for the sky. They seem to have boundless energy.

This boundless energy is readily directed to playing games, running races and participating in sports. All that this energy needs is just a little direction. Toddlers Train organizes an Annual Sports Day. Teachers think up the most amazing races appropriate for each age group. Here are some samples:

The youngest children race as 'Cookie Munchers'. When the whistle blows, the race begins and children run in their respective tracks to where the cookies await them; they munch and eat them fully and then run to the finishing line. In another race, they demonstrate that 'We Like it Clean and Tidy': each child runs to the basket lying on his track, picks it up, then runs to a pile of trash which is lying on his track, he picks it up and places it in the basket then moves forward briskly to the finishing line. Note that even a race can be designed to teach good habits to children – and they sure learn quickly.

Somewhat older children show us how to take care of themselves when they are feeling cold: each child runs on his track to a cap lying on it and puts it on, then runs forward to a muffler lying on the same track and wraps the muffler around his neck and then runs to the finishing line.

The oldest children, about age 3-plus, take great delight in exhibiting their dexterity: squatting they move on their tracks, to a rod lying before them, they pick up the rod and hop to a plastic bottle into which they insert the rod, then, holding the bottle up, they run to the finishing line.

In yet another race, they walk backwards to a tyre lying on the track, turn around, raise the tyre to a vertical position and then roll it all the way to the finishing line.

Well before the Sports Day comes round, the children begin to rehearse the particular race they will be running; they understand that they are to stand behind the starting line until the whistle blows; that they are to stay in their own track; that they have to do each bit that characterizes the race; that they have to focus on what they are doing and not be distracted by what others are doing; that if someone is ahead of them or behind them is of no consequence; that what is important is to run the race correctly and complete the race all the way to the finishing line and that is what they have to do on the Sports Day.

Each child learns at his own pace and runs the race at his own pace and that is totally acceptable to the teachers. The teachers' mandate is to teach the children to run the race by the rules all the way to the finishing line. As the children improve with practice, they are told so. In effect, each time they run, they are competing with themselves in terms of how they run this time compared to how they ran the last time. And when they run the race right, they are the winners – each is a winner and every one of them is a winner.

On the Sports Day, as the parents, grandparents and siblings make themselves comfortable in the audience stands, all excited and hopeful that the child they are rooting for will excel and win all the races, the Master of Ceremony addresses them and advises them that in the races that they will soon see, every child is a winner, and insists that we clap for all the children including the one who reaches the finishing line last because that is what is important: that the child ran the race right all the way to the finishing line. There are no first or second or third prizes, continues the Master of Ceremony. Every child will be given a prize – the same prize because every one of them is a winner. The assembled spectators are requested to treat everyone as *the* winner.

So that the parents of children who do come first, second and third are not deprived of their thrill, the Master of Ceremony explains that we do have a victory stand, and children who come first, second and third will be taken to the victory stand and will step up to take their appropriate positions and the photographer will click their pictures which will be made available to the parents. So have fun.

And, everyone has fun for here is a Sports Day where every child is a winner today and because of today, will be a self-confident, *whole* person tomorrow.

Shantanu Flips

SHANTANU, just about 4 years young, was a 'heavyweight'. In relation to other children in his class, he weighed one-and-a-half to two times as much. His extra bulk slowed him down. When others hopped, he flopped. When others crawled into the space below the table and then crawled out with ease, Shantanu followed them, but ended up dragging the whole table with him, thanks to his upward-protruding bum! That he was not as agile as his friends was becoming apparent to him. He enjoyed the pranks that children amuse themselves with but for each new antic, he had begun to 'weigh' the consequences, vis-à-vis his own weight, before attempting to indulge himself. Sometimes he would put in the extra effort that his bulk demanded and follow suit; sometimes he would desist and limit himself to just watching, instead of participating. Teachers observed that 'just watching' was beginning to win over 'participating' a bit more than was good for a child. Then the day of reckoning arrived.

Teachers were preparing the children for the Annual Sports Day. An acrobatic feat that children just loved performing, and the audience loudly applauded, was the 'Flip'. Flipping consisted of a child holding the hands of an adult as he climbed up the legs of the adult and when the child's feet reached above the adult's knees and on the adults thighs, still holding the hands of the adult, the child would rotate himself over with his legs over his own head and then, after a circular movement, land feet-foremost on the ground. Every child hesitated initially when being taught to 'Flip' but loved it when he successfully learnt to Flip.

Shantanu saw the Flip being demonstrated and was amazed by the feat. When asked to try it, he ran away. When caught and asked again to try it, he began to cry. When urged further, the crying became louder and louder.

So here was a situation.

Given his bulk, given his hesitancy to try, given that his crying was getting louder and louder, was it wise to persist or wise to 'let it be' and let Shantanu not learn to Flip and not take part in this event.

'Let it be'! Not being able to Flip is not the end of the world. It is not good to make a child cry. One should not force the child. The child could be scarred for life. '*Let it be.*'

Or by 'letting it be', are we, the adults, reinforcing his fear and opening the door to let in more fears? Will this teach him to use his tears as a means of blackmailing and getting his own way out of a tricky situation?

No, 'let it be' is not the right way. It is the easy path. We must choose the path that empowers the child even if that path means more work for us and initially more resistance from the child.

Given Shantanu's weight and bulk, teachers needed a strong adult to make him do the Flip. The teachers available were not strong enough, so the School' s handyman was called in to play the adult's role. Two teachers positioned themselves on either side of Shantanu to help him. Shantanu was continuing to resist and cry. The teachers guided him to lift his feet and place them on the adult's legs, they spoke to him lovingly, they encouraged him, they cajoled him and then it finally happened. For a split-second, Shantanu became quiet – it dawned on him that he had actually Flipped; then the inertia prevailed and the crying resumed. The teachers clapped, hugged him and began to get him ready for the Flip once again. Shantanu's resistance diminished a wee bit and he chose to make just a little effort. With less wailing, he Flipped again. More claps and hugs. The teachers then called in some children to watch Shantanu Flip. He Flipped and the teachers clapped and asked all the children who had watched to clap. The crying stopped. One more Flip and then the lesson was temporarily halted. The handyman was sent aay to continue his usual work. The School day progressed. When it was time for the children to go home, Shantanu's driver was called into the School and Shantanu and the handyman demonstrated the Flip to him. Then the driver was asked to take the handyman's place and continue to get Shantanu to practise the Flip at home.

Next day, when the driver escorted Shantanu to the School in the morning, there was a discernable difference in

Shantanu's walk. His gait was quicker, his stomach may have been sucked in a bit – one couldn't really tell – but one thing was for sure: Shantanu's chest was definitely pushed out and there was a smile of achievement on his face. He ran to his teacher and boldly announced, 'I can Flip – wanna see?' and he began to hail his driver who was hurrying away, but returned upon hearing Shantanu call. The Flip was demonstrated yet once again and it was perfect! There was much clapping and rejoicing and Shantanu enjoyed being the centre of adulation.

Clearly the decision to *not* 'let it be' was the wise one.

Sometimes, even the most joyous stories have a flipside and this fantastic Flip story does have a flipside to it too: on his way out, Shantanu's driver was heard complaining to the teacher, 'Last evening, Shantanu did not give me a moment's peace. Flip, Flip and more Flip. I could not sleep at night – I was aching all over.'

The School is Ready When Your Child Is

THE telephone at Toddlers Train rang. 'My daughter will be turning two in four months,' the caller said. 'I am calling to find out if admissions are open now, and if not, when will they open?'

'We don't have any specified admission period,' answered Rashmi. 'We admit children when they are ready to come to school and if we have space to accommodate them.'

'Do you have space right now?'

'We will have space in ten days when two children, twins, will be leaving the School – their father has been transferred to Mumbai.'

'May I come and meet you tomorrow morning at 9:30? My name is Mrs Suman Grover.'

'Yes, indeed you may. See you tomorrow morning, Suman. I am Mrs Rashmi Gulhati.'

Children must not be kept waiting. It does not behove us to erect artificial barriers in their growth path. This is what we believe in and that is why the admission process at Toddlers Train has been designed to be flexible.

Each child is different – is unique. The pace at which each grows is different. One wants to play with other children at age two, another at two-and-a-half. One is toilet-trained at two-and-a-half, another at three. One can assemble a complex jigsaw puzzle at three, another at three-and-a-half. We must see to it that each child continues to grow at his own pace. He could learn something new each day. What that something is, is the child's choice, according to his interest and aptitude. We need to be there to encourage that learning, so that the child progresses, and to ensure that the child does not get hurt in the process.

Joining a play school is a novel experience for every child. No longer is the daily environment limited to the home with occasional visits to random places and also sometimes to the same places for regular visits, accompanied by mom, or mom and dad, or other familiar adults. Going to play school is different – it is a repeated visit to the same place and one that is specifically and solely for the child. Different children react differently to it. On the one extreme is the child who walks into the school with alacrity, with a smile on his face and who immediately gets immersed in all that the school has to offer. On the other end is the child who begins to cry the moment he senses that this means a parting from his parents, and clings on to them. The child has to be pulled away and brought, crying, into the school premises, and then the teacher, on a one-to-one basis, has to help the child to stop crying by diverting his attention and luring the child onto something that he relates to. The child calms down but the calm is temporary and soon the child is back to crying. The teacher initiates a new activity; the child stops crying; and then after a while begins crying again. It requires great patience and ingenuity on the part of the teacher to get such a child acclimatized to his new surroundings.

Most children, of course, do not espouse either extreme and behave anywhere in the entire range between the extremes. Typically, a child will walk into the school holding the teacher's hand, sensing its warmth, attracted by the novelty of where he is walking into and indulges his natural curiosity to discover whatever there is to discover. After a brief exploration, the child remembers the parent and misses that particular affection and then begins to cry. The crying can be subdued by providing the child with a new interest or object of curiosity. If this ploy succeeds, the child continues his time in School. If not, the child is brought back to the parent who has been advised to wait nearby for a while. The process is repeated for a few days with the time spent in School increasing each day and then the child is set to stay in School until it closes for the day.

There is yet another interesting child-behaviour that is manifested by some children. After a few days of attending school for the full duration, comes a morning at home when the child is reluctant to get ready to go to school and the parents are totally confused as to why. They had thought the child was done with his initial hang-ups and reticence. The child has, in fact, merely wanted the morning to be different. Parents of children joining Toddlers Train are forewarned of the possibility of the occurrence of this behaviour and are advised to display 'firmness with love' that rapidly takes care of the situation and the child agrees to get ready and go to school.

And then, finally, the child adjusts to a new pattern in his life. A pattern that is in fact going to be set until the child grows up to be a teenager. The 'firmness-with-love' treatment by the parents comes in handy throughout the child's schooling period. As no doubt, all of us will recall as we look back to our own lives, there were those days when we just did not wish to go to school, and depending on how strong the wish was, we came up with excuses. Most of these excuses did not, in fact, cut much ice with our parents except when we feigned that unverifiable terrible headache!

PART II

THE GLOBAL REALM

A Child is Born

TODAY you are reading this Book. Today about 370,000 children will be born in the world: 70,000 in India; 50,000 in China; 16,500 in Nigeria; 12,000 in Indonesia; 11,000 in USA; 8,000 in Brazil; 4,000 in Uganda; 3,600 in Russia; 3,000 in South Africa; 2,800 in Japan; 2,000 in UK; 1,100 in Canada; 800 in Australia; 200 in Switzerland; the remaining 185,000 (50 per cent) will be born in the other 182 countries of the world. These are just estimates since many births are not registered. Each of these children is unique. Each has arrived with a potential whose worth is unknown to us but it is our responsibility to ensure that that potential is allowed to develop to the maximum extent possible – otherwise what is the point of bringing a child into this world?

Let us consider one of these children born today – one who is born in China – let us say a girl child. In 1980, China had adopted a one-child policy with minor exceptions. Only in 2015, it has been decided to phase out this policy. Let us say that the girl child in question has been born in a region where the one child policy still continues. This girl child is therefore so precious to her parents! She is the one and only one for them. Her mother was also the only one for her parents and so was her father, the only one for his parents. This newborn is the only grandchild that her maternal grandparents will ever have. So also for the paternal grandparents. For six adults – parents and two pairs of grand parents this new born is the one and only one. One cannot conceive of this child lacking love. Most likely she will have an abundance of it – from six doting adults. She will no doubt thrive in this loving atmosphere where every wish of hers is instantly catered to, maybe even before she expresses it. There may be some child, a rare one, who may find this doting adult environment a bit oppressive.

Let's look more closely at the world from the viewpoint of this newborn girl: she will never have any siblings, nor any cousins, nor any uncles, nor aunts, only parents and two sets of grandparents, all adults, two one generation older and four two generations older. She will have no relative of her own generation to play with, to fight with, to laugh with, to grow up with. And this is sadly true of nearly every child being born in China. It is all the consequence of a law the policy-makers in China put into action about three-and-a-half decades ago so as to control and slow down the growth of a very large population. A population so large that it was believed it was hindering the country from developing economically.

Did someone give any thought to the millions of children that would be born without siblings? According to Vinita Nangia, in her article, 'Little emperors, China's precious snowflakes!' in *The Times of India* of 12 May 2013, 'China is saddled today with a generation of spoilt brats called "little emperors." One sees them all around – brattish, self-centred and selfish, a generation focused on itself and caring little for others.' This girl-child born today is 'lucky' that she was not a victim of female foeticide – a phenomenon that has resulted today in there being 120 young men for every 100 women. This may generate in this girl-child a feeling of exclusivity as she grows older. Parents of young girls have 'high expectations of their sons-in-law, and some are even demanding dowry! A young girl's much publicized recent confession on a television talk show says it all – "I would rather be crying in a BMW than laughing on a bicycle!".' The single-child policy of China has succeeded in controlling the population and boosting its economy but it has, as Vinita Nangia quotes Paul French as saying, also produced a generation that he describes as, "'precious snowflakes' wrapped in cotton wool from day one. Nothing is quite right for them. It is always either too hot or too cold and they are all hypochondriacs. They get immediately stressed out if they have to lift a finger." Continues Vinita Nangia, 'Indeed by 2050, … China (will be) losing its most precious commodity, a young, willing workforce, innovation and dynamism will soon be a thing of the past, wiping out the entire golden story of the rise of the Chinese dragon.'

China has now begun, reports Vinita Nangia, 'moves to backtrack on the one-child policy in a phased manner'. It is amply apparent from this account that taking a decision on account of 'national interest' and imposing it on the population of the country may safeguard the national interest under focus but it can also alter the entire nature of the population and with time become a new liability for the nation. This debate is now getting hotter: *The Economic Times* of 13 February 2015 reports that Mei Zhiqiang, the deputy director of the Family Planning Commission in northern Shanxi province said, 'We should make sure our policy and system allows our children to give birth to two children...and they must have two children'. The report continues, 'Some lauded Mei's suggestion, calling it an assertive way to rectify the maladjusted demographic structure. Others sniffed at it, criticising it as another compulsory policy, state-run Global Times said.'

Let us consider another child born a week before, a boy child born to a very well-to-do couple in India. He is their fifth child – Baby 5. Baby 1 was born eight years ago – a girl. Baby 2 was born six years ago – a girl. Baby 3 and Baby 4 were born two years ago – twin girls. Today, the parents have organized a big celebration on account of the birth, finally, of a son. Champagne will flow, conches will blow, the mother of the son will glow and the father of the son will get to show (show off, that is). Baby 1 is confused by the euphoria she has witnessed during the last week. Two years earlier, when Baby 3 and Baby 4 were born, there were only a few congratulations passed on and they were whispered ever so softly, as though they were uncalled for. Baby 2 is delighted – she is now six years old and she is being allowed to pick up and hold Baby 5 and cuddle him and play with him – she had not been allowed to do so when she was four years old when Baby 3 and Baby

4 had arrived. Baby 3 and Baby 4 are puzzled because they are no longer getting any attention. Having a son is very important to most couples in India. And if you don't succeed in the first try, then try and try again and for some – keep trying until you do.

For this couple, their one son arrived after four daughters. The parents will dote on him and will teach the sisters to dote on him and unless wisdom dawns somewhere along the line, the world will have one more brat in its midst. Why is the birth of a son so important for so many in India? Much of India has a patriarchal society. It is not politically correct to state what I am going to state but this is what the tradition has brought many to believe. The son keeps the family name going. In a joint family, the son remains at home. The son is there (supposedly) to look after the parents in their old age. The son is there to light the funeral pyre when the parents die and that is believed to be auspicious.

The daughter is a guest at home – she leaves when she gets married. And she *must* get married and she *must* leave – in the ceremonial *doli* (transporting her in a decorated carriage) from her impermanent home to her *real* one, the husband's, taking with her ample dowry so that she is welcomed in the home of her husband and in-laws and not hang around in her parents' home all her life and leave only upon her death in the *arthi* (departure of the carcass on a wooden board from home to the cremation ground). The daughter is a liability; the son is an asset. Such beliefs have lead to the evils associated with dowry and at the extreme, to female foeticide. It has led the Government to draw up laws against dowry, for strong punishment to perpetrators of dowry deaths and to bar revealing the gender of an unborn child.

But one cannot pass laws for everything and for some that have been passed there is no way to ensure that they are implemented. Many a parent will leave no stone unturned to get their son admitted into a prestigious school whereas be quite content at whichever school the daughter makes it to. Providing the son with useful stimuli is very important; the daughter can help her mom around the house—those are the only skills she'll need, anyway, in her future home. That 'I am special' attitude soon gets engrained in the son and he goes about pushing his sisters around and gets away with it. And, a male chauvinistic society thrives.

Let us now consider a child born today in the U.S.A. to a reasonably well-to-do urban couple. Even before the child, let us say, the first child and a girl child, arrived, the baby's room had been set up and furnished. Friends had organized a surprise 'baby shower' for the expectant mother to be showered with gifts for the baby: toys, pink-hued clothes, a pram, a car seat, a rocker, lotions, bags of disposable diapers, a baby monitor and on and on and on. Upon getting home from the hospital where the child was born, the baby will have a gaily decorated crib to sleep in, her very own special tub to have her bath in, her very own wardrobe with appropriate attire and on and on and on. And the on and on and on will continue as the baby grows older: at each age, suitable new toys, new clothes, new activities, new exposure, new experiences. Also, new wants: 'Mom can I have this, and also that?' to which the answer usually will be 'Yes, dear.' and she gets this and that: a new entrant into the consumerist society – 'you are most welcome!'

Finally, let us consider a child *about* to be born today somewhere in the world to a young couple who are in the category known as 'below the poverty line' (BPL). They live in a dilapidated small shack with a leaky roof. It is located in a colony of similar shacks beyond the outskirts of a town. Each morning, groups of men and women make their way to the town in the hope of getting a day-job and those that don't get one, trudge disappointedly back to the shack-colony in the afternoon, and those that are lucky enough to land a job, get back late in the evening. The BPL couple who are about to have a baby live by themselves in this colony. They too head out each morning to the town notwithstanding that the young girl is expecting - they need a daily wage just like the rest. For the last three weeks, the BPL wife has not been able to take the trip to town. She is in her ninth month of pregnancy. As in the last few days, today again, she is lying on her mat on the floor as her husband heads to town. As the morning progresses, she feels some discomfort. Then suddenly the pain strikes and she yells out - not just because of the pain, but to alert any neighbour who is within earshot to come to her aid.

Two women enter the shack and seeing the girl's state, one runs out to seek out the woman who is known in the shack-colony as the 'wise' one. She has been with many pregnant girls in the shack-colony when they were about to deliver. She is not a trained midwife – just a 'wise' lady. She comes in now with the woman who had gone to find her. They do what they believe has to be done. In mid-afternoon the child arrives – a boy. There is much relief and joy to share.

Soon thereafter, the 'wise' one leaves, as does one of the two women. The other remains until the BPL husband arrives. The BPL couple marvel at their newborn, they thank God, they gaze at each other and at the baby, but soon it was time to stop gazing and to get on with the chores. The husband has to do them today. The next day, the husband will have to skip going into town for work. The day after, he will resume going—he has to.

What lies in store for this baby boy as he grows up? Food – just a minimal amount. Good health – unlikely, on account of malnutrition and lack of sanitation. Good care – hard to come by. Not long after the baby's arrival, the BPL couple will begin to feel the burden of their double income having been reduced to single income and with the added needs of the baby, they will keep searching for someone to leave the baby with so that both of them can go to work.

The baby had survived his birth. Would he last for a month under such circumstances, and not become yet another statistic for neonatal mortality? Would he last a year and not be a victim of infant mortality, would he live for five years and escape the period of child mortality and thereafter, would he actually grow up to adulthood? The data are revealing. As per the World Bank's findings of 2013:

Country	*Neonatal mortality no./1000 per year who did not survive*	*Infant mortality no./1000 per year who did not survive*	*Child mortality no./1000 per year who did not survive*	*Total*
Somalia	46	90	146	282
Pakistan	42	69	86	197
Nigeria	37	74	117	228
Afghanistan	36	70	97	203
India	29	41	53	123
China	8	11	13	32
U.S.A.	4	6	7	17
Japan	1	2	3	6

Although this data are for the countries cited as a whole, one can safely assume that within each country the contributors to its mortality rate are by and large those from below the poverty line. So the chance that the BPL child would not live to grow up to be an adult is about 30 per cent in Somalia; 20 per cent in Pakistan, Nigeria and Afghanistan; 12 per cent in India and less in China, U.S.A. and Japan. Those that survive, would barely survive. They may receive some love, but are not likely to receive much guidance, exposure or stimulation, and their growth would be consequently quite stunted.

Of the four babies, three who arrived today and one who arrived a week ago, the first three will have parents who can arrange to make substantive inputs to their respective offspring. What form or shape these inputs will take, depends on the society in which they live, its beliefs, their own intellectual growth, their own understanding of how crucial the first 6 years are for the growth and brain development of a child. But the fourth baby, born to the BPL couple with lots of nothingness around him, will never have the opportunity of having his potential blossom. What is particularly tragic is how high the percentage of those living below the poverty line in the world is. The statistics, as per the World Bank based on 2011 data, paint a grim picture. The figure is the worst for the Sub-Saharan Africa region where 47 per cent of the population is below the poverty line and the percentage for South Asia is 25 per cent. Just these two regions have 80 per cent of the 1 billion people in the world who fall into this category.

Attending to children in the crucial period between 0 and 6 years is no doubt the duty of the parents, but it is also the duty of the government of each nation. How each of them is attending to this duty is discussed in the next two chapters.

Private Initiatives

THE well-to-do always have options. If the mother is inclined to look after her child herself, she will organize things so she can do just that. If, before the child's arrival, she was a housewife, she will employ house-help to take over the tasks she had attended to in the house so that she will have time to devote to the child. If she was employed, she will take long leave or quit her job and employ house-help suitable for her requirements. If she wishes, by and large, to carry on with her earlier pursuits, she will engage a nanny to look after the child or enrol the child in privately run day-care centres.

At each age of the child, he will be provided with a variety of stimulants. There will be toys that tickle his senses: generating sounds and introducing the child to beat and melody; the battery-operated ones that perform and provide a visual treat. Then those that require assembling and have been designed to generate creativity and dexterity. Then, the kind that are directed more at developing comprehension - which items in a row are similar, which different, and so on.

Storybooks, picture books, scribbling pads, painting books, play dough will make their entry when the child is ready for each. Slides, swings, jungle-gyms, merry-go-rounds, trampolines, tricycles will be provided to develop motor skills. Television programmes will engage the child when the mom needs a breather, and then will follow i-pads, and more.

Mothers will network with other mothers and playgroups will be created and the children will learn to socialize and play games: hide and seek, follow the leader, golf, football, cricket and hockey. Children will be taken to classes to learn music, drama, dance, ballet, pottery-making, painting.

Is there a limit to all this? For loving, devoted mothers, there is none. They have loads of enthusiasm, ingenuity, imagination, energy, persistence to do what they believe is good for the development of their children. It is the enlightened well-to-do who are able to give their children a stimulating environment and that is what enables the children of such well-to-do to do well when they grow up. In their childhood their parents did all they could to make their brains grow.

The private sector has made major in-roads to provide facilities for pre-school care and education.

There are neighbourhood schools, whose quality depends on the person who set up the school – some are good and there are others that could be much better, and yet they all provide a service to those who live in the neighbourhood and do not have the resources or time or understanding to seek out better options that might not be so conveniently located.

There are schools that are set up by someone who has the passion and knowledge to offer the highest quotient of advancement to a child. Their reputation travels way beyond the neighbourhoods in which they are situated, and caring parents bring their children to them from all over the city.

And then there are schools set up by entrepreneurs who look upon child education as a business opportunity. Such schools are designed to attract parents. They have good infrastructure, well-appointed play fields, attractive toys and learning materials, colourful walls and inviting furniture. Presumably, they also have good teachers and methodologies but these are not immediately visible to the parents. Nevertheless, many a parent gets hooked-on by their visual appeal. They flock to such schools because they advertise themselves extensively and well, promising the 'best' one for their children. Many such schools are good, and care about providing quality, but because they are primarily business ventures, they care most for the bottom line: the profit the school makes.

Such a business thrives when it has not just one school but a chain of them all over town. They thrive through brand marketing. All the branches would have the same kind of learning resources and facilities but clearly they would be different since they would have different teachers – all seemingly good but not necessarily so. After all, their jobs and salaries are also dependent on the bottom line of the enterprise, and that is a major concern along with, hopefully, a concern for the children in the school.

Some ventures, after making a name in one city, head to another one. Others more enterprising head to different countries as well. The brand begins to count and yield returns. As per *The Times of India* of 16 August 2014, the story titled, 'Modern Montessori to expand pre-schools in India' states:

> A Singapore-based education group is planning to expand its reach in India by doubling pre-school teacher training and franchises for running kindergarten classes through major corporations… 'We feel there is this huge demand in India for trained pre-school teachers and demand for kindergartens in cities,' said T. Chandroo, chairman and chief executive officer of Modern Montessori International (MMI), an education brand from the UK... MMI presently runs 10 pre-school teacher training centres and five kindergartens in India, having first forayed into the Indian market in early 2003.
>
> 'We are going to serve the concept to more corporations,' Chandroo told PTI… He stressed the need to train pre-school teachers based on an estimated demand for 100,000 such educationists over the next 10 years… 'We are looking at opening up another 20-30 centres in the next three to five years,' Chandroo said, listing out Bangalore, Chennai and Mumbai as the starting-off points for both teacher training centres and pre-schools… MMI also operates in Sri Lanka, Thailand, Vietnam, Indonesia, Nigeria, Kenya, Egypt, Nepal and Hong Kong. 'But there are huge opportunities in India's education sector,' Chandroo reiterated.

If one Googles for information on the Net, say for play-schools in Delhi, there are more than 1,600 options to choose from; for playschools in Washington D.C. there are some 600 options to choose from – and, oh yes, you can choose also by indicating how much you are willing to pay. In the U.S. figures run as high as $30,000 a year. There are many international schools teaching in English in Beijing, in Tokyo, in Dar-e-Salaam, in fact, any and everywhere in the world.

How does one go about choosing a school? There are the obvious constraints: location, expense, transport, timings, but even with constraints there are often choices. One can be bowled over by advertisements, brand names, reputation, as well as by "so and so's" who are sending their children to that school, "so it must be good" Some parents are also on the lookout for schools where one gets an opportunity of net-working with the 'who's who' outside the school gates when you go to pick up your child and all are waiting for the school to get over. What counts and is important for a parent depends on each parent.

One can also get professional advice in relation to 'what to look for in a school'. The Washington D.C.-based National Association for the Education of Young Children (NAEYC), 'the world's largest organization working on behalf of young children' on its website, has plenty to offer. It lists '10 standards for early childhood programs that can help families make the right choice when they are looking for a child care center, preschool, or kindergarten. The standards and criteria are also the foundation of the NAEYC Accreditation system for early childhood programs.' Each of the ten standards has 3 to 5 issues that are addressed, resulting in a total of 41 criteria for assessment. Out of the 41, only 8 are highlighted below:

- Teaching staff engage in warm, friendly conversations with the children and encourage and recognize children's work and accomplishments.

- Children are encouraged to play and work together.
- Teachers help children resolve conflicts by identifying feelings, describing problems, and trying alternative solutions. Teaching staff never physically punish children.
- Children are given opportunities to learn and develop through exploration and play, and teachers have opportunities to work with individual children and small groups on specific skills.
- Teachers modify strategies and materials to respond to the needs and interests of individual children, engaging each child and enhancing learning.
- A variety of materials and equipment appropriate for children's ages and stages of development is available and kept clean, safe, and in good repair.
- The facility is designed so that staff can supervise all children by sight and sound.
- Outdoor play areas have fences or natural barriers that prevent access to streets and other hazards.

Parents owe it to their children to pay heed to such good advice, seek out a pre-school that gives importance to what is relevant and important for the development of their children and not be taken up by the glitter and glamour that some pre-schools are good at shining in their eyes because the pre-school's managements eyes are focused primarily on their bottom line – their profit.

Public Policy and Its Implementation

A. Introduction

U.S. President Barrack Obama in his 2013 State of the Union Address proposed:

> 'Study after study shows that the sooner a child begins learning, the better he or she does down the road. But today, fewer than 3 in 10 four-year-olds are enrolled in a high-quality preschool program. Most middle-class parents can't afford a few hundred bucks a week for private preschool. And for poor kids who need help the most, this lack of access to preschool education can shadow them for the rest of their lives.
>
> 'Tonight, I propose working with states to make high-quality preschool available to every child in America. Every dollar we invest in high-quality early education can save more than seven dollars later on—by boosting graduation

> rates, reducing teen pregnancy, even reducing violent crime. In states that make it a priority to educate our youngest children, like Georgia or Oklahoma, studies show students grow up more likely to read and do math at grade level, graduate from high school, hold a job, and form more stable families of their own. So let's do what works, and make sure none of our children start the race of life already behind. Let's give our kids that chance.'

Is it not shocking that even in the United States of America 'fewer than 3 in 10 four-year-olds are enrolled in a high-quality preschool program'? But perhaps one can begin to hope: this was probably the first time that 'our youngest children' found a spot in an American President's State of the Union Address. This 'first time' may be so because what had happened three years earlier, as described hereafter.

B. World Conference

Also, for the very first time ever, in 2010, there was a world conference held in Moscow devoted solely to our youngest children, organized by the United Nations Educational, Scientific and Cultural Organization and the Russian Federation known as the 'World Conference on Early Childhood Care and Education (ECCE): Building the Wealth of Nations' with an overall theme: 'ECCE as the first and foundational step for building the wealth of nations'. The Conference was attended by about 1,000 delegates from 193 countries. Its Concept Paper highlights:

(i) the now well-established benefits of ECCE
(ii) the current state of affairs relating to ECCE in different nations
(iii) the challenges that continue to retard the progress of providing ECCE

Each of these three are considered briefly below:

Benefits

(a) Good health and nutrition for the expecting mother and during early childhood, positively influence the child's 'cognitive function, psychomotor development, fine motor skills, activity levels and attention span.'
(b) Participation in pre-school programmes 'can improve school readiness, and nurture positive self-image and learning dispositions... It makes enrolment in the first grade of primary education more likely, and increases retention, completion and achievement'.
(c) A very significant influence of ECCE is that it 'helps level the playing field for disadvantaged children as they enter primary school, empowering them to be confident and successful in later education and employment'.
(d) Policy-makers always have their eye on the expense involved in providing any facility. In this regard, many studies have conclusively shown that the cost-benefit ratio is very favourable 'since children with quality ECCE experience tend to advance to higher education, obtain employment,

have higher earnings as well as savings, provide higher contributions to social security, and are less likely to be on public assistance and commit crimes'.

Current State of Affairs

In recognition of these benefits, some progress has been made in equitably enhancing provision of ECCE globally during the last three decades but the primary focus of most nations continues to be to achieve universal primary education. 'The global pre-primary gross enrolment ratio (GER) increased 7 per cent, from 33 to 40 per cent between 1999 and 2005.' In terms of numbers this increase amounts to 20 million children but it still leaves ten times this number, i.e. about 200 million children, who are bereft of this care in the most important period of their life. The 7 per-cent increase is mostly because of improvement in the situation 'in South and West Asia (76 per cent), sub-Saharan Africa (61 per cent) and, to a lesser extent, Latin America and the Caribbean… However, GERs in Arab States and Sub-Saharan Africa remain below 20 per cent… The two regions account for almost three-quarters of the fifty countries with GERs below 30 per cent'.

Challenges that Retard Progress

(a) A weak policy framework – Only about 80 countries legally recognize early childhood as a period for the first stage of the education system. Even among these, many focus only on the age group of 3-6 ignoring the needs of 0-3-year-olds. There is more rhetoric and less implementation and this is amply evident from the fact that 'In most developing countries less than 1 per cent of the total education budget is allocated to early childhood programmes, and even when health expenditures are included, the allocation remains small compared to other education sub-sectors'.

(b) Inequitable access – The disadvantaged continue to be at a disadvantage. In most countries, the rural and the urban poor lose out. In less developed and developing countries, large percentages of children lose out even more acutely. Only those with wealthy parentage have the private sector catering to children's needs.

(c) Quality disfavours the poor – Public schemes that supposedly reach the stage of implementation leave much to be desired including trained teachers, reasonable teacher-student ratios, adequate physical facilities and educational resource material. 'The lack of training on early childhood pedagogy often results in ECCE staff using a didactic, teacher-centred approach which is not suitable for younger children. It may also lead pre-primary teachers to over-emphasize the acquisition of academic skills and give less consideration to promoting social, emotional and physical development.'

The Final Report of the Conference, along with many other futuristic plans and hopes, calls

(i) upon UNESCO to 'Champion holistic ECCE at national, regional and international levels based on the principles of children's rights…(and) Work closely with Member States, UN agencies, civil society, specialized agencies, partners and experts to develop holistic integrated ECCE programmes, with particular attention to children aged zero to three'.

(ii) for harnessing of resources 'by increasing budget allocations by all government departments concerned with the promotion of ECCE, and mobilize diverse and innovative financing sources and mechanisms in support of ECCE. Invest sufficient resources in ECCE to meet set quality standards and enable all rights to ECCE'.

(iii) for empowering and strengthening 'the capacity of parents families and service providers, so that they can provide protective relationships, quality care and education to the young child… [and] Improve curricula and methodologies in tune with childhood, valuing play, affection, cooperation, talent and creativity, joy, the fostering of self-confidence and autonomy, as well as active learning pedagogies that take into account a child's point of view'.

World conferences are great for focusing attention on what is or should be considered important. Statistics presented at these conferences are great to highlight what exists and what one needs to work towards. The conference ambience is great for noble thoughts to be enunciated. Once the world conference is over, delegates return to their countries – to what exists there, and with hopes to improve and move ahead.

What public policies are currently in place in different countries is an eye-opener and we will delve into them, hereafter focusing specifically on an opulent country – U.S.A., at an overpopulated country – China, and a futuristic country – Japan.

C. In the United States of America

President Obama's concern for the country's youngest children is well founded. According to Zero to Three, a National Centre for Infants, Toddlers, and Families, the country has about 12 million children under the age of 3. Almost half of them belong to low-income families. In terms of relative child poverty, children of USA rank last among 20 economically most advanced nations. Growing up in low-income families impinges negatively both on the nutrition and health care of these children as also on their brain development, with consequences that affect their entire life. There are many Federal support programmes, such as, Medicaid and Children's Health Insurance Program (CHIP), Supplemental Nutrition Assistance Program (SNAP), Special Supplemental Nutrition Program for Women, Infants, and Children (WIC), Temporary Assistance for Needy Families (TANF), Low Income Home Energy Assistance Program (LIHEAP), Early Head Start (EHS), Child Care and Development Block Grant (CCDBG) and more. Unfortunately, their reach is limited. For example, only 27 per cent of families with children receive TANF benefit; CCDBG is able to serve only about 16 per cent of the eligible children; less than 4 per cent are able to take advantage of EHS, and so, sadly, on.

A House Budget Committee Report, 'The War on Poverty: 50 Years Later', released on 3 March 2014, described numerous schemes in operation and funded by the Federal Government. The Head Start Program is one scheme of relevance to the youngest children. This scheme 'gives grants directly to local public and private non-profit and for-profit agencies to provide early-learning and development services for low-income children from birth to age five.' The Report raised issues about the benefit of the programme. Two days later, on 5 March 2014, Katie Hamm, Director of Early Childhood Policy at the Center for American Progress, presented a critique of this Report and stated, 'Current investments in early childhood are grossly underfunded. At current funding levels, the Head Start program reaches just half of all eligible preschoolers, and Early Head Start reaches 4 percent of eligible infants and toddlers... The average cost of a child care center varies by state but reaches $16,000 annually for an infant and $11,000 for a 4-year old'. In regard to issues of benefits raised by the Report, Katie Hamm observed that, 'Where they have failed, it is because the federal government has not invested resources to support broad access to quality programs.' Clearly, the problem is not just that the programmes are lacking in quantity but that they are also lacking in quality. Katie Hamm concluded, 'Our approach should be to bolster and improve these programs.'

In 2013, EHS was funded to serve only 3.5 per cent of the approximately 3 million children who were eligible to participate. In 2014, EHS funding was $1.37 billion and was expected to serve 4.5 per cent of the eligible children. Not a big deal.

And that is not all. According to a study carried out by CATO Institute in Washington D.C. and reported by Tad DeHaven in September 2010, 'A lot of the funding on federal and state social welfare programs never reaches recipients because it is consumed in paperwork and improper spending. And government aid often goes to people who don't really need it...funds are distributed to local governments and private-sector grantees. Unless granted a waiver, grantees must contribute a 20 percent funding match. Grantees can use up to 15 percent of a program's total costs for administration... The formula for allocating Head Start funds is very complex... Convoluted funding formulas in grant programs generate bureaucracy and encourage interest groups and politicians to battle to get a greater share. Federal aid allocations often reflect political pull, not relative need across different communities... The groups that receive Head Start subsidies are often wasteful managers, and some groups blatantly cheat federal taxpayers. In 2000, the Government Accountability Office found that 76 percent of Head Start grantees reviewed were not in compliance with financial management standards... News stories have revealed outright fraud among Head Start recipient groups.

In Maryland, the Head Start director was arrested on charges that she stole $335,777, and in South Dakota a woman was prosecuted on charges that she embezzled $185,000 from a Head Start program.'

One can only hope that the interest and wishes of President Obama will initiate a much-needed massive change, and that the youngest citizens of the most opulent country in the world will have the opportunity to develop more fully as they grow.

D. In China

The single-child policy in China, makes each child a great treasure to possess. Apart from pampering, there is also an enormous urge to care for the child.

Monica Lysack, the then Executive Director of Child Care Advocacy Association of Canada, on a study tour to China in the year 2000, was surprised to discover that there was substantial difference between her expectations and reality (http://www.ccaac.ca/pdf/backgound_docs/Early_Childhood_Care_and_Education_in_China.ppt.). Instead of small and crowded facilities, over-structured and teacher-directed programmes with inequities due to gender and income she had expected in the institutions she visited in Beijing, she found well-designed facilities, well-trained and well-respected teachers, high-quality programmes accessible to the majority of families irrespective of income. Chinese society clearly values its children and takes care to nurture them in a fashion that current knowledge considers appropriate, as was apparent from the Montessori influence that was clearly discernable. The fact that each child had no siblings was specifically addressed by encouraging the children to 'cluster' and interact with each other. She returned thinking that Canada could learn some from China. Well, more like from what was the situation in Beijing, not necessarily in the rest of China.

And, according to a story in the *China Daily* of 27 November 2010, titled 'China Strives to Lift Preschool Education', 'Preschools are the "weakest" part of China's education system, according to the Chinese government, which says it will generally improve the country's kindergartens to ensure a quality start for children.' The problems identified included, 'lack of teaching resources, inadequate investments, understaffing, underdeveloped management systems and imbalances between urban and rural areas'.

The Chinese government considers education as the key to development and has given it great importance. As per a survey reported by China Education and Research Network, by the end of 2002, there were 111,800 kindergartens and four times as many primary schools, numbering 456,900. The junior secondary schools numbered 65,600 and the senior secondary schools were 32,800. Nine years of compulsory education had been universalized in the area inhabited by 90 per cent of the population. Higher education has also made remarkable progress with 2003 institutions having an enrolment of 16 million students.

However, in the midst of all this expansion and development, preschools did not get sufficient attention. As per the *China*

Daily report, 'local governments did not attach enough importance to preschool education, citing that government-spending on the issue only made up 1 percent of total education spending'.

The year 2010 proved important for the youngest citizens in China. The process had begun two years earlier, in 2008, at the Chinese People's Political Consultative Conference (CPPCC) where the view was that development of education must be treated as a priority for modernization of China. It was decided to develop a national plan for education (2010-2020). Premier Wen Jiabao himself headed a group for the purpose of formulating the plan. According to Xin Zhou of East China Normal University, in his article *Early Childhood Education Policy Development in China* published in Korea Institute of Child Care and Education's International Journal of Child Care and Education Policy 2011, Vol. 5, No.1, p. 29-39. 'Eleven thematic panels were formed, involving nearly 2,000 people and more than 500 scholars and experts. The central government has made it clear that education is a major issue of public concern in China and all plans should be widely discussed with the public in an effort to seek consensus.'

The Plan 2010-2020 formulated states that 'early childhood education is critical for young children's health, habit formation and intellectual development. Early childhood programs need to acknowledge children's developmental nature, use scientific teaching methods and ensure that children develop in a healthy and happy manner.' The Plan acknowledges the fact that providing for early child education is the responsibility of the

State and to do so it must enhance the financial resources for it and ensure that towns and cities include this as an integral part of their development plans. More specifically, it declares, 'Program standards and licensing requirements need to be established. Teacher qualification and the overall quality of the teaching staff could be enhanced by professional development. Teachers' salaries, status and treatment need to be ensured by law.'

For better implementation of the Plan, the China State Council issued a document specifically directed at early education which identifies many relevant issues and considers them in greater detail. Of particular interest is the recognition it gives to the unique manner in which education for the very young has to be organized and the need to monitor its quality: 'Early education should follow children's developmental characteristics, education for all children as well as pay attention to individual child. Play should be treated as the main activity in the program, combining care and education, since children learn through a variety of activities and in an enriched learning environment. An effective early childhood program quality monitoring system should be set up.'

The Provincial Governments have reacted very positively to this concept of focusing on early education and they in turn required that each county prepare a 3-year action plan along a format that was provided. The result was clearly amazing in that most provinces came up with goals for 3-year enrolment by 2015 that were higher than the national goal specified in the Plan. Some goals pronounced were that 'By 2015, Guangdong province will provide compulsory ECE education for all children. Shanxi province will start one year of free education for children aged 5-6 from September 2011. Nanjing will start free education plan for all children aged 3-6 in the city, including for the children of migrant workers'. Along with higher goals came specific proposals for organizing in-service teacher training, identifying institutions where pre-service teacher training programmes would begin, paying better salaries to teachers and providing other incentives as well for those willing to go to teach in rural areas, etc. There is clear recognition of the difficulties that will have to be faced: the most important ones being to come up with sufficient number of teachers swiftly, and ensuring that the focus on achieving the requisite numbers not sacrifice quality for quantity.

Implementation of ambitious plans always comes with accompanying challenges. Success comes only when these challenges are effectively addressed and tackled. But foremost, there must be belief in the desirability and necessity of achieving the goals. Fortunately, for the youngest children in China, and then subsequently for all of China, it appears that the realization that one must focus on the very young is happening rapidly.

E. In Japan

Ever since 1947, Japan has been running two types of institutions for children in the 0-6 years age group. Of these are the *hoikuen*, that is, day-care centres. They are administered by the Ministry of Health and Welfare (MHW). The other is the *youchien*, that is, kindergarten, administered by the Ministry of Education (MoE). Hoikuen are centres that cater to children from birth to 6 years and look after the children for about 11 hours per day for 300 days a year. They have to have kitchen facilities. Clearly, they are of special significance for working parents who are unable to give their child the care he needs round the clock. The youchien are for children in the age group of 3-6 years and operate for only 4 hours a day and for 29 weeks in the year. Their focus is on early childhood education and, as can be readily deduced, cater to parents who are able to provide personal care to the child and are looking only for educational inputs. The article, 'The Japanese Preschool System in Transition' by Yuke Imoto of the University of Oxford, published in *Research in Comparative and International Education, Vol. 2, No. 2*, 2007, stated that in mid-2005, there were 23,000 hoikuen with 1,990,000 children enrolled in them, and that there were 1,400 youchien with an enrolment of 1,740,000. As per http://www.country-studies.com/japan/primary-and-secondary-education.html, the Ministry of Education's 1990 Course of Study for Preschools is followed both by hoikuen and youchien and focuses on language, expression, human relationships and the environment. Some 58 per cent of youchien are run by the private sector and they cater to 77 per cent of the children enrolled in these institutions. Together, hoikuen and youchien enrol over 90 per cent of all children below 6 years of age. Clearly, the youngest citizens of Japan are not only well cared for but are provided with worthwhile educational inputs. As Mariko Ichimi Abumiya, Senior Researcher, National

Institute for Educational Policy Research, Tokyo, said in her paper *Preschool Education and Care in Japan* (ref. http://www.nier.go.jp/English/educationjapan/pdf/201109ECEC.pdf), in Japan 'A very refined and holistic concept of *hoiku* (care and education) has been used for more than 130 years. It can be said that hoiku is originally almost equivalent to ECCE or ECEC, and it is strictly and carefully distinguished from *gakko kyoiku* (school education) because early childhood developmental needs are quite different from those of school-aged children.'

Unlike most countries where policy-makers have only recently begun to recognize the importance of attending to children in the age group of 0-6 years, Japan not only recognized that this was a crucial period for the development of the child, but also made a concerted effort to establish institutions that provided relevant inputs to the children. Yuke Imoto had said, in 2007, 'officials sought knowledge around the world to establish effective educational systems. The ideas of the German educator Friedrich Froebel, the founder of the international kindergarten movement, were introduced into Japan along with a vast array of other Western educational ideas during this time... and in the Fundamental Code of Education proclaimed in 1872, kindergartens... were included in the system.' The initially set-up kindergartens, both private and public, were directed by Westerners or those who had studied abroad, but it took only a generation to recognize that all that Western influence was not what Japan needed or wanted and the curricula was redesigned to suit the Japanese national identity, focusing on values such as discipline, good habits and respect for parents. These *youchien* catered to the children in the 3-6 years age group.

In the early 1900s, these youchien were found not to be the appropriate institutions to fulfil the new needs of those of the Japanese population that had begun to shift from rural to urban areas to take advantage of job opportunities that emerged on account of rapid industrialization. Children in the age group of 0-3, who had been traditionally looked after by their mothers, and sometimes by extended families, had no one to look after them, because mothers had become keen to work outside the home and earn and the extended families had broken into nuclear ones.

According to Yuke Imoto (2007), charitable institutions came to the rescue of these young ones as they set up what came to be known as *hoikuen* that functioned 'for long hours and during holidays, and attention was given to children's physical development as well as their mental and moral development'. And, after about four decades, in 1947, the 'Child Welfare Law placed the hoikuen as an official institution under MHW jurisdiction… and transformed the day-care centre from a charitable system of protection to a "right" for all young children to receive care and attention.'

Hoikuen and youchien have since the middle of the twentieth century coexisted, serving the changing needs of the Japanese population: for example, in order to cater to the post-War baby boom, the number of hoikuen jumped from 783 in 1946 to 3,684 by 1950, overtaking the youchien, that numbered 2,100. As the years passed, the scenario in Japan, as indeed all over the world, kept changing. Economical development needs led to diminished funds for hoikuen. Well-to-do women, professionally employed, did not wish to spend all their time bringing up children. This resulted in lowering the birth rate in Japan – so much so that it became a national concern. The private sector began to invest in setting up hoikuen and youchien catering to market needs, and their roles began to get mixed up, especially that of the youchien which began to cater to the needs of mothers who wanted their children to be looked after for longer periods. Attempts to amalgamate the two ran into difficulty in the form of a turf war between the two ministries, the Ministry of Health and Welfare pushing the imperative need for child care, and the Ministry of Education highlighting the importance of education. Come 2006, the Japanese Government initiated the establishment of a new type of institute, the *nintei-kodomoen,* that is, 'accredited children's centres' endowed with the kind of flexibility required in current times: catering both to child care and education; for age 0-6 years; functioning for 4 or 8 or more hours; with kitchen facilities if appropriate and necessary; and with a fee to be set by each institution individually. The market mechanism became the guiding light. Each nintei-kodomoen is designed to cater to the community and neigbourhood where it is located. Through this innovation, the Japanese Government recognized the need to cater to the development of the children and simultaneously to the needs of the parents, to the national need for a higher birth rate and, of course, to save government funds where they can be substituted by private funds.

E. In Conclusion

Governments of nations across the world have been largely ignoring children in the age group of 0-6 years. As noted earlier, the World Conference on ECCE 2010 reported that in most developing countries the early childhood programmes got a paltry 1 per cent of the education budget. In China as well, as we have seen, government expenditure on these children was just 1 per cent of the education budget. The situation in the high-income countries that belong to the Organisation for Economic Co-operation and Development (OECD), is better, but even there the youngest in their population get a raw deal: under the heading 'What share of national wealth is spent on education?', in *Education at a Glance 2014*, http://dx.doi.org/10.1787/eag_highlights-2014-18-en, 'Spending on pre-primary education accounts for nearly one-tenth of spending on educational institutions, or 0.6 per cent of the GDP, on average among OECD countries. There are large differences among countries. For instance, spending on pre-primary education represents less than 0.2 per cent of the GDP in Australia and Switzerland, and only about 1 per cent or more in Denmark and Iceland.

The good news is that one can see that a change is in the offing as is evident from what has been presented herein vis-a-vis the stories in the U.S.A., China and Japan. Although scientific development and studies have been highlighting the importance of nurturing children in the 0-6 age group for quite some time now, its significance has just begun to be appreciated by policy-makers in these countries. Governments in different nations inevitably have different and complex problems to deal with. In some places and/or at some time, the birth rate is too high, or too low; too much of the population is in the working age group, and/or is too old; government funds are needed for providing subsidies to the needy and they are also needed to generate economic development. There is need to focus on developing infrastructure, on industry, on agriculture, on healthcare, on education and so on. Each government has its worries about its nation's security and about defense-preparedness; about natural disasters and its capability for their management and so on. Each nation, each government, each political party has its own philosophy about how much to focus on what and when, on how much to cater to the short-term and how much to the long-term and so on. Each nation has had its high points and its low points. No one has come with a formula that works at all times and at all places. It is time to come up with a new strategy.

Perhaps the new strategy and a winning one would be to spend more time, more effort, more money on the 0-6 age group children. The inputs made during this time period are what really counts, since this is the time when the brain is formed. By making the appropriate inputs one can ensure that the children have good values, good habits, good intellect, good skills and that is what will ensure that they grow up to be good thinkers, good workers, good individuals and good citizens. This sounds not only good and promising – some thing that is well worth trying – because it is logical. The nation that takes this thought seriously, gives it the highest priority, focuses on it, and acts on it effectively, may well turn out to be the most successful nation in the world.

What is the scenario in India? What is the policy? What is on the ground? What needs to be done? For answers, we come to the next, the last part of this Book.

DELECTABLES II

Mr Wilson and *Sab Ka Nana*

DOES it not strike you as odd that Dennis the Menace calls Mr. Wilson—'Mr. Wilson'? After all Mr. Wilson is a familiar neighbour and Dennis is such a frequent visitor at his home! But then, America has a culture different from ours. Dennis is a kid and he has not been brought up to call the older gentleman anything other than Mr. Wilson. When my own teen-aged niece and nephew, who live in America, following the practice prevalent there tried to call me by my first name – Shashi, I was taken aback and quickly put my foot down. No 'Shashi' for me. Call me 'Mamaji'. And as a major concession, I relented and let them call me 'Shashi Mamaji'.

We are different here! The other day, at Ansal Plaza, Rashmi had to go to the loo. She handed me her purse and I waited outside in the corridor. As I waited, I observed a young man also waiting with a purse in his hand. So I commented to him, 'Looks as though we are engaged in identical jobs.' He must have noted the purse in my hand and he laughed and said, 'Yes, Uncle' and just then, his wife came out of the ladies toilet and, seeing me with her husband, gave me a pretty smile and they took off. And as they did so, the young man turned to say, 'Bye, Uncle'.

For our xeroxing work, I began to go to a particular shop in a market near our home. Most others who come there are errand boys, peons and the like. As is my habit, I get my work done and pay up and then thank who ever has attended on me. After a few visits, they began to recognize me. After a few more visits, they began to take greater care while doing my work. After some more visits, I began to be greeted with, 'Uncle*ji aaiye, aap kaise hain aaj* (Come in, respected Uncle, how are you today*)?'*

I am sure you must have experienced, as indeed I have, that when you step up to ask a stranger in our country for information—on directions, assistance, or whatever—you get a far better response if you begin by addressing the person with a '*Bhai ji* (respected brother) or *Behan ji* (respected sister)'. I am convinced that if Dennis the Menace were to begin addressing Mr. Wilson as 'Uncle', Mr. Wilson would transform from a grumpy old man who thinks Dennis is a nuisance, to an indulgent and avuncular figure who might actually begin to find Dennis cute.

Let me relate an incident that gave me one of the greatest thrills of my life. There was a time when Toddlers Train was run on the entire ground floor of our house, where we lived on the first floor. I had to go down often on some errand or the other. Actually, going down and seeing the toddlers do their thing was extremely rejuvenating, and after working for a while, it provided a most welcome relief to take a trip down to the

School. On one such trip, before the School day had begun, I passed through a classroom to go to the backyard. There were two 3-year old young men there who had just come to that classroom and were placing their tiffin boxes and bags on the rack. On my way back from the backyard, one of the boys was still in the classroom. Turning to me, he said: '*Pranav kehta tha aap Nana ho* (Pranav says you are maternal Grandfather).' and I asked '*Kiska Nana hoon main* (Whose maternal Grandfather am I)?' That gem of a child answered, '*Sab ka Nana* (Everyone's maternal Grandfather).' Given that Rashmi and I have two sons and that I am never going to be a biological *Nana* – I feel so blessed to be '*Sab ka Nana*'.

I do hope, that as we come together globally, one day Mr. Wilson will be called 'Uncle' by Dennis.

Policeman to the Rescue

TWO kids and a toy.

Says Kid-1, 'I want to play with this.'

Says Kid-2, '*I* want the toy, *I* want to play with it.'

We have a problem.

We urge the kids to take turns. 'Okay,' concedes Kid-1, 'but I'll play with it first.'

Says Kid-2, implacably, 'No, *me* first.'

We still have problem.

We suggest tossing a coin. Says Kid-1, 'No, I must play first. I'm the one who found the toy.'

Says Kid-2, 'I will play first. It is *my* toy.'

The problem persists.

We advise Kid-1, who is a little older, to let the younger one Kid-2 have a go at it first. Says Kid-1, 'No, I'm older, I get the first chance.'

The problem continues.

We admonish Kid-2 that since the toy is his; he has played with it often; it is good to share one's toys, so let Kid-1 play first since he has never played with the toy before.

Says Kid-2, 'No, I have not played with the toy for such a long time because I could not find.'

More of the same problem.

We try again and point out to Kid-2 that the lost toy was found by Kid-1, so he should be grateful to Kid-1 and let him play first. Kid-2 has run out of arguments, and so he begins to cry and yell, 'I want to play first!'

No further dialogue is possible. Kid-2 tries to grab the toy. Kid-1 resists and a fisty-fight begins.

Sure sounds familiar, doesn't it? There is no universal solution that can be prescribed. Each such situation is different and calls for a unique solution. All situations do eventually get resolved but don't have equally happy results for the parties involved. Our grown-up attempt, of course, is to avoid making them unhappy, avoid being coercive; we have to be ingenious.

Here is what I witnessed one day in Toddlers Train, and did I find it ingenious? No, it was much more, it was fantastic!

Three 4-year-plus-olds were playing in the garden. They were having tons of fun. They were being very inventive, and the games they played had no known names. The kids were not just enjoying playing, but clearly they were enjoying each other.

To add to the fun, Rashmi asked the maid to take the bicycles out from the garage so that the children could ride them in the driveway. The children saw the bicycles arrive and were thrilled: new activity means a different, new kind of fun. There were, however, only two bicycles. All three wanted to ride. Obviously one could not. They would have to take turns. Which two get to ride the bikes first? Which one has to sit out?

No one wanted to sit out. Oh, oh, problem in the making! Had Rashmi's idea of getting the bikes out misfired? I wondered. It could have been a massive dampener of the children's spirits had Rashmi been short of ingenious ideas – but that was never the case.

And so, said Rashmi, 'Okay, two of you will ride the bikes and the third will be a policeman. This is the policeman's pedestal where he will stand and when he holds his hand out like this, the bikers have to stop and remain stationary, and when the policeman turns and holds his arm spread like this, the bikers can move forward. Now, who wants to be the policeman?'

Two hands went up. Rashmi then decided who would be the policeman first and her decision was immediately accepted. All choices had their advantages, so the problem dissolved instantly and to everyone's satisfaction and the fun began.

What Happened? What Happened?!!!

CHILDREN have enormous energy, and they are constantly putting it to use—although not always with happy results. They run, they climb, they jump, they hide, they seek, they play, they laugh, they talk, they yell… and then you hear a shriek….

Ever so often, a child quite suddenly, starts to cry.

Sometimes, it is apparent as to 'what happened': the child fell down, someone pushed the child, someone snatched away the toy that he was playing with, and so on and so forth.

One does not need to ask 'What happened?'; one knows or can safely guess. One also knows how to remedy the situation.

If the child upon falling down is physically hurt, one attends to the injury, and when the pain diminishes, the child ceases to cry.

If the child has been pushed by another, one admonishes the pusher and helps to negotiate peace between the pusher and the pushed.

If the toy has been snatched away, one recovers the toy, and again focuses on the snatcher to ensure that the snatcher behaves better in the ensuing interaction.

But there are occasions when it is not apparent as so why a child starts suddenly to cry. One has not seen the child fall or get hurt, or anyone pushing him, or snatching away a prized toy.

And that is when one needs to ask 'What happened?'. The child will usually respond instantly: he will point towards the hurt, or accuse the pusher, or demand the toy back. And again, one can take immediate action to redress the situation and put an end to the child's tears.

But mysteriously, there are occasions when a child begins to cry and when one asks 'What happened?', all one gets for a reply is more crying, and even louder crying.

What does one do then?

Insist on getting an answer and so keep on repeating 'What happened'? Tell the child that he is being silly and should stop crying? Admonish the child that unless the child tells one the cause of his crying, one cannot help him? Scold the child and tell the child to stop being silly and crying for no rhyme or reason? Shake or slap the child for making a racket, and bark at him to shut up? Probably, none of these actions will work, nor are they warranted.

Why does the child not reply and explain why he's crying? Is the child just being obstinate, is the child just ruining your peace for the heck of it, is the child over-anxious to get your attention, or what? How does one explain such behaviour?

How does one react and respond effectively to incessant crying? This is the question I posed to Rashmi and she responded:

'My experience tells me that one should not keep asking "What happened?" Instead, one should just hold the child, hug him close, show him how much you love him, make him feel safe and cared for. The crying will soon subside. Then distract him with something that he enjoys and the crying will gradually cease altogether, and he will begin to behave like a child always does – with plenty of energy, and with more energy to spare.'

Why does this work, I questioned? And, Rashmi answered:

'Perhaps, because the child himself does not consciously know the reason for that episode of crying. Something happened, something was said, something was unusual, something was different – it placed him in a situation that was unfamiliar, unpalatable, unacceptable – but he was not quite able to consciously recognize it for what it was, and so he just burst into tears, uncontrollable tears. So, the holding, the hugging, the loving gradually transports the child back to the normal, the usual, the palatable, the acceptable, and he revives his spirits. It is not uncommon, that after some hours, even after some days, he will remind you of the incident of the crying session and give you a reason for the crying because the reason finally dawned on him as it moved from the subconscious to the conscious.

'Adults, when feeling depressed, are known to sob their hearts out in the darkness and silence of the night, and sometimes the tears spill over and become visible to someone who cares for them– they too can only be revived by holding, hugging and loving by someone who cares for them. Children also need to be held, hugged and loved by someone who cares for them when something upsets them and they know not what.'

My Name is...Enjoy the Show

DO you think you could have, when you were about three years old, walked on to the school's stage, to its centre, where a mike had been placed, and said a few words all on your own to a large and gaping audience of parents, grandparents and similar kin sitting on chairs, and a whole bunch of young children, perhaps also your older siblings, fidgeting around on carpets just in front of the stage? Only you know the answer.

At Toddlers Train, every child in School does this and has been doing this for decades at the Annual Cultural Programme that the children put up. Under the item 'PRICELESS GEMS from our LOVELY GEMS', each 'gem' walks to the mike and begins with 'My name is…' and then tells the audience something about himself – what he likes to eat, who his best friends are, what he wants to grow up to be, or where he went on his last vacation. Or he recites his favourite poem, sings his favourite song, or whatever had been the gem's choice and had been rehearsed to say on this occasion, and then, having said all this, the gem concludes with 'Enjoy the show', waves a goodbye and returns to the green room. These gems are just priceless – at just about three years of age.

Very, very rarely does it happen that a gem is rendered dumb with stagefright and fails to carry on. When such a thing *does* happen, a teacher moves onto the stage and kneels supportively behind the child, and with a little prompting, the gem recovers his voice. He begins to say 'My name is…' and concludes cheerily with 'Enjoy the show!'.

The Annual Cultural Programme has always proved to be an amazing event. Children enact a play, give life to a song, imitate a character, dance to lyrics that have been specially written for them, along with music composed and played in a manner so that they can respond to it with vigour and passion.

At the very outset, Rashmi sensitizes the audience, informing them that the programme has been designed not for their entertainment but for the children's all-round development. That is not to say that the audience will not be entertained, but that the said priority is crucial. Fortunately, here, both parents and teachers have the same priority: our children.

Rashmi recently told an eagerly listening audience:

> 'The past few weeks have been challenging stimulating and as we progressed, most satisfying for all of us. This evening, you will see the culmination of our collective effort. This effort is collective, and yet it is an effort that is different for each child because each child is different. As we structure this evening's production, we keep in mind the physical,

emotional and mental temperament of each child and build on their individual innate traits, talents and capabilities and make inputs that will foster multi-level and multi-faceted development for every one of them. We use this evening's performance as a tool to help children to develop self-esteem, to blossom and to gain confidence. We are not seeking perfection but focusing on providing the children a happy and fun-filled opportunity to develop new skills, to learn to work in harmony with others and to enjoy being an integral part of a satisfying whole. We use it as a tool to develop creativity, presence of mind, a spirit of adventure and the capacity to cope with the novel and unfamiliar. These capabilities become apparent when the children are older, but the seeds need to be sown now.'

Rashmi then cautioned them,

'Today, our children need our appreciation and encouragement. Let us give it to them in ample measure with many rounds of thundering applause. The children are likely to amuse us a lot, but let us restrain our laughter, since children do not always interpret laughter as appreciation but often as "being laughed at". Please do not call out to or wave to the children—that would be too distracting and may unsettle them.

Later, when the children join you, please do not compare them to others. Appreciate the effort they have made and build up their self-esteem. This will reap more than ample benefit in the time to come.'

Parents and children both remember this special event and what they experienced during it for many, many years. Several parents, when they run into Rashmi at social events in town, refer to it and trace some achievement of their now grown-up child to this experience.

Usually at such events, schools invite some important personality to be the chief guest. Toddlers Train never succumbed to following such a practice. They did not consider this occasion as one for showing off the School's capabilities to the chief guest, nor the School's relationship with the chief guest to the parents. It believed that the presence of an eminent personality would be distracting – diverting the attention of many away from the children, and onto the eminent chief guest. For Toddlers Train the chief guests were always the children – at the Centre of its Universe.

Tiny Steps to Big Leaps

ARJUN and Sidharth are first cousins and live together in a joint family. They are about the same age – Sidharth just a couple of months older. They joined Toddlers Train together and became classmates. They would come to school together brought by either one's mom or dad, and of course be picked up by them to return home together

Upon reaching in front of the School, Arjun would hop out of the car and in through the gate in a big hurry and rush into his classroom to deposit his tiffin box there, and would then emerge out of it rapidly so that he could get started in whatever play activity that was engaging the children who had reached School earlier that morning. Sidharth would enter the gate slowly, carefully minding others who were in the driveway, walk slowly into the classroom and take his time to come out of it. He would then look around, hesitating over which path to take, and then move to some place from where he would watch – just watch - the others play. Only after receiving some encouragement from a teacher, would he join others in some play.

Be it outside in the play area or inside in class, Sidharth was a reserved person. Arjun was not only full of energy, but also active in displaying it. The former had to be constantly nudged and the latter sometimes restrained. The markedly different personalities of the two cousins was an enigma that needed probing.

Sidharth's mother provided the clue. Both the boys were tiny images of their fathers. Sidharth's father was the first child of his caring parents and was a few years older than Arjun's father. As often happens, caring parents' over concern for their firstborn leads to the child developing an inhibited personality. By the time, the second child arrives, the parents are more relaxed and not so overprotective and the second child becomes more confident since he is not advised all the time to be careful and is allowed to proceed on and embark on initiatives he wishes to follow up.

What Sidharth needed was, therefore, not just to be nudged into action but to be helped to feel self-confident. A strategy to achieve that was formulated and put into action.

The next day in class, children were assembling jigs-saw puzzles and the teacher showing them how to do so. When the teacher finished making her puzzle, she softly requested Sidharth to put her assembled puzzle on the shelf near the wall. He hesitated and the teacher motioned him to come forward. He got up quietly and came and carefully picked up the puzzle and took it and placed it on the shelf, and came back to his seat. The teacher quite loudly thanked Sidharth for so carefully placing the puzzle on the shelf.

He must have been pleased to be thanked but he did not show it.

The following day, when the children finished playing with a bat and a ball, the teacher asked Sidharth to pick up the bat and the ball and take them to the class and put them in the bin where they were stored. He did. The teacher made sure that her acknowledgement to Sidharth was heard by all the children in the class.

Each successive day, the teacher commissioned Sidharth to do something she needed done and what had to be done became more and more complex and complicated. Sidharth did, did it well, and was duly acknowledged. Gradually, everyone in the class began to rely on Sidharth to attend to work that had to be done to streamline the activities being undertaken in and out of class. Sidharth looked forward to his daily tasks and in due course began to attend to them without being asked. That his classmates began to depend on him, and looked up to him, was all heading towards building up Sidharth's self-confidence.

Three months later, Sidharth's mother reported that he had begun to take the initiative in attending to many things at home. The need for nudging had markedly diminished. He was becoming more explorative. A month later, she reported that he was not following Arjun around all the time but inviting Arjun to join him in activities he had thought up himself to engage in.

In School, it was amply evident that Sidharth's posture had changed. His shoulders were pushed back and his chest had become more prominent. He emerged out of the car each morning more purposefully, not jumping around as much as Arjun, but with resolve and alacrity. Sidharth developing self-confidence indicated a big leap headed to growth – a leap that began with just a tiny step, but a tiny step with a well-conceived strategy, with a design and a purpose that was executed subtly but with persistence.

PART III

THE NATIONAL REALM

For the Youngest Citizens of India

THE youngest citizens of India, in the age group of zero to six years, numbered 158.7 million in the 2011 census, that is, 13 per cent of the total population. They found a place in the Constitution of India only in 2002, more than five decades after the Constitution came into effect, through amended Article 45 (The Constitution Act, 2002) which directs that '*The State shall endeavour to provide ECCE for all children until they complete the age of six years.*'

ECCE, that is, Early Childhood Care and Education, first received some mention in the National Policy for Children in 1974. The priority therein was on issues of health and nutrition. As regards education the Policy states, '*The State shall take steps to provide free and compulsory education for all children up to the age of 14*' but for the youngest citizens of India it only added, '*The programme of informal education for preschool children from such (weaker) sections will also be taken up.*'

It was only in 1992, after the revision of the National Policy of Education (1986), that the young ones in India in the age group of 0-6 received four small paragraphs of attention. Here are excerpts from these paragraphs:

> 'The National Policy on Children specially emphasizes investment in the development of young child...'
>
> 'Recognising the holistic nature of child development, viz., nutrition, health and social, mental, physical, moral and emotional development, Early Childhood Care and Education ECCE will receive high priority and be suitably integrated with Child Development Services programme...'
>
> 'Programmes of ECCE will be child-oriented, focused around play and individuality of the child. Formal methods and introduction of the 3R's will be discouraged at this stage...'
>
> 'A full integration of child care and preprimary education will be brought about both as a feeder and strengthening factor for primary education and for human resource development in general.'

Clearly over two decades ago, the policy-makers had become aware of the manner in which young children needed to be catered to. Not formal teaching methods, not the 3Rs but play-oriented exposure and stimulation with due recognition of the requirements of each child which differ from child to child to child. Also, that one needed to invest in the young child not only for the development of the child but for human resource generally.

At this time in 1992, a 144-page long Programme of Action was formulated to implement the new Policy of Education and the preschool child grabbed 5 pages of the Programme. But so what? In 2009 came The Right of Children to Free and Compulsory Education Act. For preschool children, its Section 11 turned out to be a far more diluted version than the 1992 version; it stated '*With a view to prepare children above the age of three years for elementary education and to provide ECCE for all children until they complete the age of six years, the appropriate government may make necessary arrangement for providing free preprimary education for such children*'. Which is the 'appropriate government'? And, if it is a 'right' why does it say 'may'?

Formulating correct and relevant Policies and Programmes of Action are essential prerequisites to making desirable changes. But unless action is initiated and relentlessly pursued, no change occurs. Ground realities remain the same. What are the ground realities in India today? To comprehend them, one has to recognize that there are three players in action: the private sector, the non-governmental organizations and the government itself.

The private sector caters to those that 'have'. The 'haves' have the money, the resources, the desire, the ambition and the inclination. They also have the understanding of the importance and the need to have inputs made into their young children although they do not always have the understanding of what kind of inputs are better than others. And, this lack of understanding is fully exploited by those in the private sector who wish to do so and they go about loudly proclaiming that they are there to provide the best inputs to the child, although, in reality, their primary concern is to maximize profit from their enterprise. But there are also plenty in the private sector with high ethics that are carefully nurturing the young ones as they should be and ensuring that the exposure and stimulation they provide lead to developing the child's numerous talents. Be that as it may, there is no shortage of choice for the 'haves' to select from and they do so with gusto.

The government has made no attempt to oversee or regulate the private sector that runs pre-schools/play-schools/nursery-schools. Some policy-makers criticize this and demand regulation so that quality education is the focus. They presume that regulation ensures quality. A very big presumption! Actually, because there are no permissions to be obtained from the government; no certificates; no prescribed fees or minimum necessary infrastructure or minimum teacher-student ratios; no inspections, there is thus no cause or room for corruption. And this has been a blessing. Institutions are available in the entire range of excellence from the best to the not-so-good and they charge the fee that they feel is right and the 'haves' are willing to pay. The 'haves' can exercise their free choice. If they make a good choice, they benefit, and if they make a poor choice they suffer - but they have only themselves to pat their backs or their bums.

As noted above, the government has made no attempt to regulate preschools but it has been busy whittling away at them – at least in Delhi. As per policy documents, ECCE is for the age group from 0-6 years, with focus on care from 0-3 years and added focus on education from 3-6 years and the Right of Education in regular schools is from 6-14 years. Education from 3-6 years is described as preschool and it is supposed to be child-oriented, focused around play and keeping away from the 3R's. Something that is best arranged in the informal environment of play-schools. Children in Delhi used to move from play-schools to regular schools at the age of about 5 years. Now they are required to move if they have reached the age of 3, as on 31 March of the current year and join the nursery class, then a year later move into the KG class and then a year later into class 1.

Clearly, moving children at the tender age of 3 plus to the formal environment of a regular school is in effect stealing their childhood from them. What is the hurry?! Where is the hurry?!! There appear to be many lobbies at work!!! Best to leave it at that. Except to note that it is contrary to the National Policy for Children (1974) and National Policy of Education as revised in 1992. This was clearly enunciated by the Ashok Ganguly Committee Report on Pre-Primary and Pre School Education in Delhi prepared at the behest of the Delhi High Court and submitted in 2007, where they state that when 'a child of 2-2½ years of age enters into a system which also has adolescents of 17-18 years of age… It defies all logic of 'child-centric' education... It is seen that, barring a few exceptions, these schools are nothing more than mere downward extension of the formal and structured education at the level of Class I and above. The unrealistic expectations of parents for early stimulation of their children and the inappropriate learning environment offered by schools staffed by either untrained or unsuitably trained teachers have resulted in a confusing and often chaotic situation.' The years of preschool for the young ones in India, even the young ones of the 'haves', have been intruded into by the inept policies of the government, and their childhood is being stolen from them as indeed their opportunity to fully develop their brains, their skills and their personalities.

Like the private sector, the second player in action, that is, the non-government organizations, has also been creating ground realities much before policy-formulation began. There have been and are innumerable individuals, all across the country, who could and can not just be silent witnesses to the plight of young children – the lack of nourishment in their food, the missing heath-care, the absence of purposeful nurturing and above all the incapacity of their parents to do anything about it. Whatever each such individual could do, he or she did—from just one's own input, in terms of time and money to the extent possible, to creating a Trust or a Foundation and involving others to put up a joint effort. This has given rise to 'balwadis' where children are looked after in terms of food, play and baby-sitting, while their parents go to earn a living. Some such endeavours reach just a few children in the neigbourhood, some go beyond and are able to reach out to hundreds of children, and a few even to thousands. The work of some of these organizations has been noticed, acclaimed and some have even been honoured with awards. There is, however, no retrievable data on the total number of children benefiting from these endeavours. It is unlikely that the number is significantly sizable. The population of children in the relevant age group is just too large, more than a million and a half. These initiatives are probably more than just a drop in the bucket, but probably not too many drops.

Government is, of course, the third player in action to create ground realities. After formulating the National Policy for Children in 1974, its first initiative, begun in 1975 on a pilot basis, was the Integrated Child Development Services (ICDS). Its objective was to lay down the foundation for holistic and integrated development of the child and building the capabilities of caregivers.

From the website http://www.aanganwadi.org/

> *Anganwadi* is a government sponsored child-care and mother-care center in India. It caters to children in the 0-6 age group. The word means 'courtyard shelter' in Hindi. They were started by the Indian government in 1975 as part of the Integrated Child Development Services program to combat child hunger and malnutrition.
>
> There are an estimated 1.053 million anganwadi centers employing 1.8 million mostly-female workers and helpers across the country. They provide outreach services to poor families in need of immunization, healthy food, clean water, clean toilets and a learning environment for infants, toddlers and pre-schoolers. They also provide similar services for expectant and nursing mothers. According to government figures, anganwadis reach about 58.1 million children and 10.23 million pregnant or lactating women.

58.1 million children are catered to in 1.053 million anganwadi centres by 1.8 million workers. In other words each centre has about 55 children being attended to by 1.7 workers. That is one worker looking after about 32 children.

At the World Conference on ECCE in September 2010 in Moscow, Dr. Shreeranjan and Archana Sharma Awasthi made a PowerPoint Presentation on 'ECCE – Indian Perspective'. Dr. Shreeranjan was then the Joint Secretary in the Ministry of Women and Child Development, Government of India. Clearly what ever he presented we are supposed to take as totally authentic.

According to the presentation, the ICDS initiated in 1975, after receiving 'varying degrees of emphasis', thirty two years later, in the 11th Plan (2007-2012) reached the 'Centre Stage of the Plan' and is 'One of the eight flagship programmes of GOI (Government of India)'. The Constitutional Commitment of 2002 has been honoured in Section 11 of the Right of Children to Free and Compulsory Education Act, 2009. This Act states, 'With a view to prepare children above the age of three years for elementary education and to provide ECCE for all children until they complete the age of six years, the appropriate government may take necessary arrangement for providing free pre primary education for such children'. The ICDS runs 1.18 million angawadis (0.127 million more than the figure on the Anganwadi website) catering to 76 million children (17.9 million more than the Anganwadi website figure). Among its 'Recent Initiatives' is listed 'Universalization of ICDS: 14 million AWCs' (Anganwadi Centres). That is about 13 million more anganwadis than the Aanganwadi website's figure of about 1 million.

Dr. Shreeranjan's presentation states that as part of the ECCE programme, each anganwadi is provided with a 'Pre-School kit of Rs 1,000 (and the) Items in the kit consist of

Flash cards for story telling
Building blocks
Stuff toys and dolls for role play
Matching and seriation cards
Dominoes
Balls
Beads and thread
Wheel toys
Masks
Colours
Small drum, etc.'

One cannot help but wonder about this 'Pre-School kit of Rs 1,000'. How many flash cards? How many building blocks? How many dolls? How many wheel toys? As we noted before, each anganwadi has some 50-plus children. Are there enough numbers of each item to be effectively used by such a large number of children? Rs. 20 worth of items per child! The wondering stopped suddenly when I read the 'PRE-PRIMARY EDUCATION IN INDIA', a brief prepared in December 2010 by Madhumita Bandyopadhyay and Jagannath Behera for Consortium for Research on Educational Access,

Transitions and Equity (CREATE), a DFID (Department for International Development, U.K.)-funded research programme consortia exploring issues of educational access, transitions and equity in South Africa, India, Bangladesh and Ghana. On the basis of various surveys including CREATE's Community and School Survey (ComSS) in Madhya Pradesh and Chhattisgarh conducted in 2008, they stated, 'The play materials in most of the AWCs (Anganwadi Centres) visited are locked up in cupboards. This seems be a result of a fairly common belief that expensive and attractive things are too precious to be handled by children and need to be brought out for display only during inspections.'

The CREATE brief has some more revealing observations:

> … 'The pre-primary education component of the ICDS programme although evident on paper is often non-existent in reality.'
>
> … 'The quality of teaching in public pre primary *Anganwadi* centres is unsatisfactory due to a lack of trained teachers.'

At the anganwadis children are looked after by Workers (AWW) and Helpers (AWH). They are usually women who live in the neighbourhood. They are paid honoraria that currently is about Rs. 5,000 per month and Rs. 2,500 per month respectively. The minimum educational qualification for the AWW is tenth class pass. An AWH should be able to read and write. Those appointed as AWW have to undergo a 30-day training programme that devotes only 4 days to educational needs of preschool children and of which only 2 days focus on how to develop children's cognitive, physical, motor, language, psycho-social and creative capabilities. How much AWW appointees can imbibe in such a short duration and then effectively use it for the development of children is not difficult to guess: clearly, very little.

Are the AWW enjoying their work? Are they a satisfied lot? Here is a glimpse from *The Hindu* of 6 November 2012:

> The members of the Undivided Dakshina Kannada (Udupi) District Anganwadi Workers and Assistants Association staged a dharna at Tiger Circle here on Monday seeking the fulfilment of their demands.
>
> G.R. Shivashankar, President of the Karnataka Anganwadi Workers Federation, said the revised timetable issued by the State government was forcing the anganwadi workers and assistants to put in two-and-a-half hours of extra work. Earlier, the anganwadis used to function from 9.30 a.m. to 1.30 p.m. But after the revision, they had to function from 9.30 a.m. to 4 p.m. The government should restore old timings.
>
> At present, the anganwadi workers and assistants received honorariums of Rs. 4,500 and Rs. 2,250 a month respectively. The amount should be increased to Rs. 10,000 a month for the workers and Rs. 7,000 a month for assistants. The harassment of anganwadi workers and assistants by government officers and supervisors must stop, he said.

Are the children attending the anganwadis benefiting and learning as they should? Here is a glimpse from *The Times of India* of 24 September 2012, datelined Bangalore:

> The Rs 3,000-odd crore that the Centre and Karnataka pump in every year under the Integrated Child Development Services (ICDS) scheme makes no difference to little Rakesh in an anganwadi, a childcare institution, in Bangalore.
>
> The four-year-old gets a bland *ganji* (gruel) and dry bread for his lunch. Has no playground to play and the centre where he comes to every morning after his daily wage parents go to work is perpetually dark.
>
> The gloomy state of childcare in Karnataka is the focus of the Justice N.K. Patil committee, which has virtually exposed the abysmal state of anganwadis. Sample this: Of the 63,377 centres meant for children below six years, only 80 have rest rooms for children and as many as 60,103 centres do not have electricity…
>
> Shockingly, while 58%, that is 36,515 anganwadis, do not have toilets, children are drinking unsafe water at 28,643 centres which have no water filters exposing them to serious health hazards.
>
> '…there is no choice for the children who depend on this water. They cannot stay for… hours without drinking water' said an ICDS worker who preferred anonymity.
>
> The committee has noted that since lakhs of children spend their crucial years in these centres before enrolling in schools… (but to little avail)…. 'Success of any ICDS

programme primarily depends on the efficiency of its frontline staff. But there are nearly 5,000 posts that are vacant,' Justice Patil said.

To see for myself, I went to visit two anganwadis in a colony of the underprivileged in Delhi. Both the anganwadis "courtyard shelters" consisted of windowless dark dungeon-like rooms of less than 7 sq. m. in area. There were about 10 children in each, keeping busy doing nothing. In one anganwadi there was a large ball resting in one kid's hands; in the other there were two plastic toys that were visible, but ignored. I asked the lady in charge if there were more toys and she pointed to the cupboard and said, 'Yes, we take out one or two at a time.' At each place there was a metal drum that contained the mid-day 'nutritious' meal. In the first anganwadi, I lifted its cover and looked in and could barely hide my disgust at the gruel I saw. This was delivered daily by some NGO who had been commissioned by the government to prepare and deliver. The quantity in the drum was far too much for the 10 children in the room but I was told that the parents of another 20 or so, who had not come that day, would come at an appointed time to take away their portion. The children spent two hours in the dark room, then had their 'meal' and then went home. Thereafter, the aganwadi worker went on her round to interact with mothers, ostensibly to discuss their and their children's health, and provide guidance. Then she had paperwork to attend to, and by early afternoon, her day was done.

I also went to an anganwadi in a village in Gurgaon. The room was not dark and was big – about 35 sq.m. The walls had posters and charts. The former with political messages about how important education is, and the latter with numbers and alphabets – sad that the chart on A,B,C,… did not go all the way to Z, nor did it follow the correct sequence for the letters that were presented. There were again only about a dozen children. Some were drawing on slates, some just moving hither and thither. Outside the room there was an open space that children could play in – it was not a claustrophobic place, unlike the ones in Delhi. It had a better infrastructure, but I doubt if very different in terms of the stimulation it provided to the children.

Whether the children benefit or not depends on the 'frontline staff' as pointed out by Justice Patil.

But who exactly are these anganwadi workers? They are women from the *basti*, that is, the cluster of homes of the underprivileged in urban areas where the anganwadi is located, and in rural areas, they are women from the village where the anganwadi is located. According to an official of Delhi's Department of Women and Child Development that I talked to, there are many applicants for the job when applications are invited. After all, the official said, 'It is a good job – right next to home, few working hours and certainly better than going to homes in the nearby colonies to clean floors and utensils, wash clothes or cook food.'

What is their capacity to make worthwhile inputs to children? Have they received adequate training for doing so?

No, not really. I went to a training centre in Delhi commissioned by the Delhi government to conduct the prescribed training programme, and the training staff there felt that the programme was not sufficient at all. It was too short, expected to cover too many diverse subjects, and little time was given to provide hands-on experience to the trainees. They said they did their best, even though the Delhi government was very tardy in making them payments for running the programme. On occasions when they visited anganwadis to see how their trainees were performing, they found what they expected: the anganwadi workers not only lacked knowledge and skill but tended to be slack; they were just passing time and collecting their honorarium which also the Delhi government did not always pay on time. Hearing all this, I felt suffocated by the negativity and I gasped as I asked, 'What can you say that is positive about all this?' And the response was, 'It is better than nothing.' Great! So all we have been doing is fighting nothingness.

Apparently, anganwadi workers are not motivated to do their job. Once they get the job they want more for themselves even though they give little to the children. They are a dissatisfied lot. Their viewpoint is expressed by the All India Federation of Anganwadi Workers and Helpers (AIFAWH). In May 2013, the Federation published a review of The ICDS Mission. It states that ICDS is hugely lacking in performance. When providing services to ensure healthy child development should be considered 'a most basic obligation of the state', it is regarded in India only as a 'scheme' that has now been 'elevated' to 'mission mode'. It is still not a regular service. Anganwadi

Workers and Helpers 'are not even designated as (government) workers because that would require that they receive the minimum wages. Instead, they are provided pathetically small monthly 'honoraria' of pitiful amounts well below the minimum wages...This not only degrades the actual workers – it also devalues the programme itself and reduces its chances of success.'

Recognizing that these days publishing a review makes no impact whatsoever, AIFAWH decided to take the issue to the street. On 21 November 2014, 23,000 women workers and helpers, all dressed in red, wearing placards and carrying banners, proceeded from Ramlila Maidan to Jantar Mantar. The rally was addressed by leaders and after making enough noise, the police was persuaded to take a delegation to the Prime Minister's Office to submit a memorandum signed by 1.64 crore workers and helpers from across the country. But alas, it appears that Ram's *lila* (magic) chose not to manifest itself and Jantar Mantar's *mantra* (a prayer that ensures the fulfillment of one's wish) also flunked.

In the proposed budget for the financial year 2015-2016 presented by the Finance Minister of India in the end of February 2015, the allocation to ICDS as per the web site accountabilityindia.in has been cut by 47 per cent: from Rs 16,667 crore in 2014-15 to a paltry Rs 8,754 crore. The reason given is that the allocations given to state governments from the Centre have been increased and hereafter it is up to the states to allocate to ICDS what they believe is appropriate. The only message that one can deduce from this is that the welfare of children in the age group of 0-6, which was rhetorically considered to be a critical input for human development (as per the National Policy on Education 1986) is, in fact, now even less of a priority than in the past.

It is worth recalling that as per the National Policy of Education, 'The National Policy on Children specially emphasizes investment in the development of young child… Recognising the holistic nature of child development, viz., nutrition, health and social, mental, physical, moral and emotional development, Early Childhood Care and Education ECCE will receive high priority and be suitably integrated with Child Development Services programme… Programmes of ECCE will be child-oriented, focused around play and individuality of the child… Formal methods and introduction of the 3R's will be discouraged at this stage… A full integration of child care and preprimary education will be brought about both as a feeder and strengthening factor for primary education and for human resource development in general.' Just perfect – could not have sounded better. And then, what happened.? A massive reduction in allocation of funds by the Central Government and with it will go the message that this is not a national priority. There are other priorities:

> 'Swatchh Bharat – a clean India'. Sure, we can work hard to clean India, but then again it will get dirty because we would not have taught our citizens, starting from the youngest ones, to not to dirty India in the first place.
>
> 'Make in India' – sure, we may be able to 'make' in India, but

'make' what? Something initially 'created' abroad? And 'make' how? Something that lacks quality? Why not, instead, teach our children, starting with the youngest, to be innovative and endow them with skills that focus on creativity and quality? And then we can first 'create' in India and then 'make' it all of the highest quality so that the world recognizes it as 'the best' because it is coming from India.

Crafting a New India

CRAFTING a new India? What is the need? What is wrong with the present India? No, no one will ask these questions. Because no one is happy with India the way it is today.

If the Census Commissioner were to seek feedback on this issue and pose the question, 'Are you happy and content with the current state of the Nation?' it would surprise the whole country if there were even a single answer in the affirmative. Oh no, on second thought, that may not be an accurate statement. There might be quite a few who would reply in the affirmative and that would be the beginning of yet another scam: '*Who was responsible for getting so many people to say "Yes"?* Clearly, someone in power or someone who wanted those in power to get a good chit engineered this.' And then: 'What was the booty/looty that each citizen who answered in the affirmative given?' And, 'Where did all the loot come from?' And then, the media would have a ball in terms of exclusive unearthing of this and that by your channel; talking points, sorry, yelling points; and, face the nation, sorry, phase the nation.

Actually, of course, no one is happy with the current state of the Nation. On a philosophic plane, there will be those who will say one should focus on the positive and not the negative. More philosophers may explain this away by stating that it is the very nature of human beings to be dissatisfied with their lot; in no place in the world will one find Utopia. And to these philosophers, the realists will loudly respond, 'Who is asking for Utopia? We realize it does not exist. But surely one should be able to get three square meals a day, clean water to drink, a roof over one's head, reasonable healthcare, and an opportunity to grow up as an educated citizen?'

Forget about luxuries, there are not even basic necessities that are available to all of us. At the same time, it isn't as though India is lost in some abyss. There is plenty happening, developing, growing, changing – only, the change is not always for the better. And even when it is, something else happens that eats into the improvement or we are unable to appreciate the improvement and build on it.

Remember the euphoria in 2002 when Metro trains first began running in Delhi? All that guff about 'world class' city and more! On 24 August 2013, *The Times of India* carried a story titled '12 years on, Metro riders care little for rules':

> '...commuters still run pell-mell at the sight of an approaching train, squeeze through the doors all at once and make a dash for the seats. They push fellow passengers, step on others' toes and shove people in the face to fit into the compartments.

But there's no denying that the Metro is a fantastic way to travel across the city. The trains are quite clean as well as airconditioned. They come frequently and on time. To make the crowds behave, Delhi Metro Rail Corporation (DMRC) has even come out with a set of dos and don'ts: stand in queue, make way for disabled people, abstain from drunken and unruly behaviour, etc. Smoking, firearms and pets are forbidden. Riding on the roof is a strict no-no, though the punishment is only Rs 50 or a month's imprisonment.

The etiquette list hasn't made much difference to the lakhs travelling every day. The rule book is thrown aside as people struggle to catch the train, especially during peak hours. Queuing? Forget about it. Standing behind the yellow line? That's asking for too much. The surge of commuters at the Rajiv Chowk station makes it plain that even the Metro guards and CISF personnel are not a safeguard against being elbowed out of the queue or having a backpack slap you in the face.

Nevertheless, 'Crafting a New India' is not a new thought. Many noble souls in the country are ceaselessly working towards creating a better India. In every profession, there are people dedicated to this cause. Be it for better infra-structure, better agricultural production, better environment, better manufacturing, better transport, better healthcare, better education, better security, better this, better that and also better governance.

For specifics, one needs only to recall the enormous effort of Anna Hazare and his team and their quest for a corruption-free country. The effort was so visible, it generated a moving momentum. However, it did not get very far, and it was assailed by some controversies. But even if a strong Lokpal had emerged out of it, one wonders if it would have made India free of corruption. The proposed solution was not one designed to develop a general state of mind in the entire population that would make it feel that engaging in corrupt practices was a manifestation of placing one's own interests above others, above the interests of one's community, above those of one's nation, and that such selfishness was abhorrent and was to be shunned. The proposed solution was only the right to punish the guilty.

But isn't prevention supposed to be a better cure than punishment? The fear of punishment in our Nation has not proved to be much of a deterrent for wrongdoing in our country. Those with selfish enough inclinations are far too ingenious to be caught, to be found guilty and then to be actually punished.

Another specific which generated an awakening of sorts was the infamous Delhi gang-rape case of 16 December 2012 and the subsequent death of Nirbhaya. A great deal was said about how dastardly the act was, about the need for ensuring safety for women, about increasing the punishment for rape, about changing the age-definition of a juvenile rapist, and on and on. Notwithstanding the pubic outcry over the incident, it is amazing to note that all the hullaballoo surrounding it since mid-December 2012 seems to have had, shockingly, no effect on subsequent rapists. And given the number of incidents of stories about rape reported in the media, it might actually appear to some of us that they have grown more frequent. Is the attitude towards women and how they are treated in our nation going to be altered by changing the penal laws and punishment or is the attitude too deep-rooted and needs to be changed by a different mechanism that impacts our value-system?

How do we go about crafting a new India? There is no strategy as of today, there is not even a resolve that we need to formulate a fresh strategy. Only random thoughts. Here are some samples of these thoughts from diverse sources.

During the 1990s, the crime rate in New York City dropped dramatically, even lower than in the United States as a whole. Violent crime declined by more than 56 per cent in the City, compared to about 28 per cent in the nation as whole. Property crimes tumbled by about 65 per cent, but fell only 26 per cent nationally. Many attribute New York's crime reduction to specific 'get-tough' policies carried out by former Mayor Rudolph Giuliani's administration. The most prominent of his policy changes was the aggressive policing of lower-level crimes, a policy which has been dubbed the 'broken windows' approach to law enforcement. In this view, small disorders lead to larger ones and perhaps even to crime. As Guiliani told the press in 1998, 'Obviously murder and graffiti are two vastly different crimes. But they are part of the same continuum, and a climate that tolerates one is more likely to tolerate the other.' One may conclude that little inputs often yield major outputs but only if the little inputs are the relevant ones.

The editorial page of *The Times of India* of 15 February 2013 carries an interview of Kancha Ilaiah, 'a political scientist, writer and Dalit activist', by Swati Mathur entitled 'Even if 10% dalit children got English education, India would change'. Mathur had posed the question, 'So you'd support continuing reservations?' and Ilaiah answered, 'The Dalit's main agenda is not reservations. My way of equality is English education. Even if 10% of our children got English education, the intellectual field would have changed. This country would have changed. My hope is education, not reservation – and I emphasize, English education.' Elsewhere in the interview, he states, 'No amount of land, jobs or money can bring true equality – only education can.... [there should be] the same language of instruction for all children – if upper-caste children are taught in English, we should be too. We're demanding the same environments and opportunities. Then after 30 years, remove reservation, let there be fair competition – dalit children will manage.'

Undoubtedly, all children will manage through competition so long as all children have access to the same environment and opportunities. That even after 69 years of Independence, we have not succeeded in providing that to all children - neither the same, nor similar environment and opportunities and that is what is holding India back. Why have we not? There we are, back to the usual reasons: lack of values, selfishness and corruption. But what is most important in what Ilaiah is saying that we lack the realization that lasting change can only be brought about through education. Education is the relevant input. Ilaiah's primary focus is on English as the language of education and in growing India this is indeed a very important factor. But what is far more important is what happens even before formal education begins. It is the environment and opportunities that we provide our children in their pre-school years that wire their brains and determine their capacities.

The Right to Education, that is currently so much talked about, is for children in the age group of 6 to 14. But, even more than the Right to Education, what we need is the Right to ECCE – Early Childhood Care and Education from the age 0 to 6; more care from 0 to 3, and more - a different kind of education from the one imparted in the formal school system, from 3 to 6. How important the preschool years are in the life of a child has been the focus of this Book. These are the years when the child's brain is crafted. Only if we properly craft the brains of our children can we hope to Craft A New India. The current buzz phrases and strategies for National Development, apart from the Right to Education also include that India has a very sizeable young population that we must leverage, that we are heading into a Knowledge Society and India must be in the forefront of the Knowledge Revolution, that we need to establish Institutes for Innovation and so on. Sure, it is great that we have a large young population but it must be a population with well-developed brains; leading a revolution in knowledge cannot be accomplished without well-developed brains and being innovative is totally a function of brain-power. So, we need to realize the importance of pre-school years and design them in a manner that empowers the brains of our children.

According to Maria Montessori:

> 'Many defects... which become permanent, are acquired because we neglect the child during the most important period of his life – between three and six years of age when his principal functions are formed and fixed.'
>
> (From Maria Montessori's book '*The Discovery of the Child*' published by Aakar Books 2004, p. 31)

Is ECCE then the relevant input?

Harvard economist Raj Chetty in 2013 was awarded the John Bates Clark Medal, often called the 'baby Nobel'. In *The Times of India* of 22 April 2013, there is a 'Question & Answer' column in which India-born Chetty's views have been sought by Srijana Mitra Das. To the question, 'Please explain your research – how exactly does a person's kindergarten class-room experience affect their earnings in life?'

Chetty's reply: 'Our research, which analysed the long-term impacts of an experiment randomly assigned to different kindergarten classrooms in the late 1980s finds that being in a better KG classroom has long-lasting effects on success in adulthood – those lucky to have better teachers in childhood are more likely to attend college, live in better neighbourhoods and are less likely to have teen pregnancies. This led us to conclude that the value of a great teacher is very large when the gains are added up over all the students she teaches over her career.'

To the question, 'Do aspects of the Indian economy interest you?' he answers in the affirmative and having focused on how little the disadvantaged groups in India have benefited in the last many years, he states, 'I think improving elementary education, rather than just college education, is likely to be a key answer to the problem.' Clearly Chetty's research findings highlight the importance of early childhood education and of the value of having good teachers.

On 26 January 2015, the Republic Day when the U.S. President Obama was the chief guest at the parade on Raj Path, *The Times of India* carried an article, 'Education is the fourth pillar of development', by Dilip Ranjekar, CEO of Azim Premji Foundation. This foundation has for about a decade been earnestly attempting to make a positive impact on the quality and equity of education in India. As Ranjekar opined, 'most education policy documents are well thought out and well-intentioned. The issue often lies with actual actions that ensure implementation on the ground. Partial implementation or implementation that does not reflect the spirit of the policy defeats the entire purpose of it.'

That the purpose gets lost was highlighted by Chetan Bhagat, an IIT alumnus, novelist and now columnist in his article, 'We The Half Educated People' published in *The Times of India* also on that Republic Day, 'So what are we doing in our rural schools, and what kind of talent are we creating?' he questioned. 'Are we simply going to celebrate enrollment and mid-day meal figures, and forget about the school's core job – to educate? Is literacy just being able to write one's name or is it at a minimum being able to read and solve basic arithmetic problems?... millions of kids and their families are being cheated and shortchanged by us… If we don't fix the problem, we will have hundreds and millions of job seeking, hungry youth with little qualification and no educated worldview in the next decade or two. If we don't want this time bomb of human mediocrity to explode on us, let us work on reforming rural education now.'

Ranjekar had said there were three priorities of action and these were the quality of teachers, the capability of educational leaders and managers and above all, 'Early childhood education: Several research studies… have shown that early childhood is the time when children need to be exposed to a stimulating, literacy-rich environment to enhance their learning capabilities. Children who experience schooling for the first time at the age of six years are clearly at a disadvantage.'

'Teaching kids to count is fine… teaching kids what counts is best' (Graffiti published in *The Times of India* of 20 February 2013). And to this, we will all say, 'Well said!' If children are brought up with implants in their brains that keep reminding them that we must look after ourselves but not at the expense of others, rather, look after ourselves and at the same time look after others; that we must obey the law since it applies equally to everyone; that we don't jump queues but wait for our turn; that we don't cross the road when the traffic signal is red; that we don't drive into a road that has a 'no entry' sign posted; that we don't cheat in examinations; that we don't steal another's coat or camera or car or anything; that we don't hack into someone else's bank account and withdraw money from it; that we help an old man cross the road; that we respect others, especially those of the opposite sex; that we don't waste anything be it food, water, electricity, paper or, for that matter, time; that we don't throw garbage anywhere except in the appropriate bin; that we must work hard and give whatever we do our very best; that we must not cut corners or advise others to cut them and we must function so as to be role models for others and so on.

Can you imagine what our neighbourhood, our workplace, our city, our state, our nation, would be like if we functioned in these disciplined and considerate ways? Can one teach these forms of behaviour to grown-ups who have grown up doing the contrary? There is enough evidence to show that one cannot. There is also enough evidence to show that what one is taught to do as a child, one carries on doing as an adult, and any time such an adult is forced to or pushed into doing otherwise, he will not be receptive to it. There is also ample evidence that if a child is introduced to, say, music, the interest continues throughout his life. The same applies to sports, to reading, to writing, to participating in discussions, and to any other skill.

As you read this, you say to yourself, *this makes sense*! Of course it does. We all know this makes sense. So why are we not being sensible? We live in a democracy so why is it that all this does not see the light of day?

Before we discuss the reasons for why all this does not readily come about, despite our being a democracy, let us learn from an exception. I refer to a news story published in *The Times of India* on 9 August 2014, 'In her first major policy announcement since taking over from Michael Gove in a cabinet reshuffle, Nicky Morgan (U.K.'s new Education Minister) stressed that toddlers should be taught "fundamental British values in an age-appropriate way" as part of a drive to protect children from religious radicals. "Public money should not be used to support any school or early-years provider that does not support this aim because it seeks to promote ideas and teachings that run counter to fundamental British values,"... Britain's nurseries are at risk of Islamist extremism, the country's new education minister said on Friday, warning that funding of early-years education providers could be withdrawn if they are found to have links with religious radicals.'

Not only does Nicky Morgan believe that the brains of young children are pliable but for the sake of her nation declared that she will not have this misused and children brought up with values that her nation considers unacceptable. Clearly, it is possible to use the scientific knowledge relating to brain-formation in a child purposefully and to instil the desired values in all children.

Yes, India is the largest democracy in the world. We are very proud of it. Every few years we hold elections and they are peacefully conducted and their results respected. Amongst past and prevailing governance systems, the democratic pattern is considered the best. It indeed has more positive characteristics than other forms of government. Elections after a prescribed number of years provide opportunity for change in the event change is believed desirable by the majority of the population. The fact that no individual can continue in an elected position without facing the electorate at prescribed intervals attempts to ensure that no one, with impunity, ignores the needs and aspirations of those he/she has been elected to represent.

Unfortunately, there is a flipside to this as well that is not often mentioned or discussed. If an elected individual has to seek a fresh mandate after x number of years, his attempt during these x years is to promote policies and projects that will show visible results within x number of years. This means that the focus of those elected is always on the short term. Some policy or project may be good, desirable, even essential to undertake, but if its results will be visible after 2x or 3x or more years, it tends to be ignored or sidelined by politicians. Politicians tend to give precedence to the 'urgent' and not the 'important'. To take up important issues and pursue them even if it is recognized that it will take many years for the effect to be felt is something that is undertaken and promoted by statesmen. Alas, the democratic system is good at producing politicians but not at nurturing statesmen! And, the few statesmen who survive are usually paid only just a little heed.

Remember Kancha Ilaiah stating that "Even if 10% dalit children got English education, India would change" and to give you an idea how long it would take for India to change he stated, "Then after 30 years, remove reservation, let their be fair competition – dalit children will manage." Amongst policies/ projects that by their very nature, have a long gestation period and get a back seat on account of shortage of statesmen are those relating to education. And within education, the ones that get the least priority are those related to our youngest citizens clearly because they have the longest gestation period. Inputs we make today to our 0-6 year olds will not be visible until these children grow into adults and that means one has to wait for a whole generation. For these inputs to make a discernable impact and change the nature of our polity, one will need five, ten, twenty batches of children who have consistently received the desired inputs. And, that means, we will have to wait for longer, even two or more generations, for the nation to transform. We have to continue to make the relevant inputs year after year after year.

I have written this Book so that each of its readers becomes a statesman and a stateswoman. We need to invest in our youngest citizens and make them the centre of our universe. They need nutritious food, a roof over their heads, access to clean bathrooms, good health care, loving guardians when parents are away from home earning their livelihoods, a stimulating environment with ample learning resources and teachers trained specifically to cater to developing their motor skills, intellectual capabilities and, above all, good values.

What our politicians, our policy makers and all of us have to recognize, realize and appreciate is that properly attending to our children is not only very important for all of us in the long run but that it is also very urgent – the longer we take to get started, the longer it will take to show results and yield benefits to the entire nation. The longer we take to get started only means that the children of today lose out. How long can we continue to ignore our children? They need our attention ***today***.

As Gabriela Mistral, the eminent poet and educationist from Chile, and recipient of the Nobel Prize in Literature in 1945, wrote in her famous poem *His Name is Today*:

> We are guilty of many errors and many faults,
> But our worst crime is abandoning the children,
> Neglecting the fountain of life.
> Many of the things we need can wait,
> The child cannot wait.
> Right now is the time his bones are being formed,
> His blood is being made,
> And his senses are being developed.
> To him we cannot answer 'Tomorrow'
> His name is Today

As is apparent from the content in this Book, many countries are making attempts or beginning to make more serious attempts in this direction. No country as yet is moving full speed (they too lack statesmen). We are told that we are fortunate that we have a sizeable young population; many countries have dwindling birth rates. Let us take the lead and begin to develop our children, not just to give us strength through numbers, but also through their capability. Let us work to really making them the nation's strength – generation after generation of citizens who are value based, innovative and skillful who will take us forward and make India the leading country in the world. Let us work not just to get *acchhe din* (good days) but for an *acchha yug* (good era).

It is not sufficient, however, to come up with slogans and repeat them *ad nauseam*. If one wants change, then one must come with a workable action plan and systematically work on it year after year. Here again, the politician can ruin what a statesman could bring to desired fruition. And, we have to be very careful. Here is an example:

With Jawaharlal Nehru's vision and the N.R. Sarkar Committee's interim report recommendation, five Indian Institutes of Technology (IITs) were established during the period 1950 to 1963. They were well conceived, thoughtfully developed, ensuring good infrastructure, highly qualified faculty, stringently selected students – 'the cream'. Over a period of a couple of decades, the results emerged: IIT alumni excelled and contributed purposefully in India, and also all over the world. IIT became a brand name. Thousands of students wanted to join IITs but only few could be accommodated. Two more IITs were set up, one in 1995 and another in 2001, to accommodate the surge of hopeful students. In 2006, about 3 lakh aspirants appeared in the entrance exam for the 7 IITs having a capacity of 4000; that is, 75 candidates for 1 seat.

IITs were in great demand but were IITs *continuing* to excel as academic institutes. Internal problems had begun to surface. Learning resources including laboratory equipment were getting outdated, faculty numbers had begun to dwindle, even the quality of students had diminished since to get admission they had to sacrifice their teenage years to mug at coaching schools. The need for positive, thoughtful, considered inputs assumed very high importance, as I highlighted in my book, *The IITs – Slumping or Soaring*, published by Macmillan India Ltd. in 2007. Our politicians as usual turned away from the important to cater to what they considered urgent and jumped into the pit for short-term gains that matter most to them. Shri Arjun Singh, the then honourable Minister of Human Resource Development proposed to reserve 27% of seats for Other Backward Classes (OBC) in addition to the existing 22.5% reservation for Scheduled Castes (SCs) and Scheduled Tribes (STs) in the IITs and other institutes managed by the Central Government. The hullabaloo that followed kept the media thoroughly busy during the summer of 2006. The crisis created by Shri Arjun Singh was sought to be resolved by suggestions that would create bigger crises. So that reservations do not diminish the seats for general category students, the suggestion was floated that seats would be suitably increased. As though increasing seats can be accomplished just by procuring and putting in more chairs. How some of those in power can be so dumb-witted is mind-boggling. The crucial problem of shortage of faculty was not just being ignored but being enhanced. And then a couple of years later – bang – the Government decided to set up 8 more IITs. For three decades (mid nineteen sixties to mid nineties) scant attention had been paid to increasing the quantity (number of seats) but the quality of what existed was commendable and then suddenly the focus switched to quantity and to hell with the quality. Why IITs were sought after was because they provided quality education – and if they ceased to provide quality education why would any one seek admission into IITs. According to *The Times of India* of 6 July 2014:

> 'The Indian Institutes of Technology (IITs), where gaining admission is said to be more difficult than entering some Ivy League colleges in the US, have had to go through the ignominy of a second round of allotments to fill up all the seats.
>
> Of the 9,711 students, a total of 9,061 have accepted their admission. A total of 650 students, who got an opportunity to study in the premier institutes, did the unthinkable this year: They refused to study in an IIT.'

About an year earlier on 12 May 2013, *Business Today* featured an article entitled, 'Is Brand IIT broken? Hasty expansion, faculty shortage and falling student standards are taking the sheen off India's best engineering brand.' Taking all the IITs together, 2608 faculty positions that is 43% are lying vacant. Is any initiative being taken to redress this situation? Has a programme been conceived and commissioned to attract qualified, competent individuals to a career in academia and fill these positions? How long will it take? Who knows! Quite clearly, it takes decades to build quality institutions but only years to destroy them. But who cares and then comes the announcement, '...I also intend to set up five more IITs (Indian Institutes of Technology) in Jammu, Chhattisgarh, Goa, Andhra Pradesh and Kerala,' said Arun Jaitley, the honourable Minsister of Finance while presenting the budget for 2014-15. In his article 'China rising, India Falling' published in

The Times of India on 6 January 2015, Asit K. Biswas, a distinguished visiting professor at Lee Kuan Yew School of Public Policy, National University of Singapore, writes, 'With the proliferation of IITs and quota system for admission, the overall quality of future IIT graduates is bound to decline, Indian politicians, for the sake of short-term gains, have killed the goose that laid golden eggs!' Please note 'for the sake of short-term gains, have killed the goose that laid golden eggs'; who has? – 'Indian politicians'!

Back now to our youngest citizens, the only ones who have the potential to bring us the *achha yug*. It is necessary to recognize that their potential can be realized only if we come up with a well thought out plan and then push ahead with it with diligence and determination. The plan cannot be the customary five-year plan – that is not the time-span that can make a difference and it cannot be one that only lists what it hopes to achieve but it must be one that also spells out how it will achieve it, who all will achieve it, where and when what will have to be done to achieve it. It will have to be an action plan – a twentyfive-year action plan – one which will need to be reviewed every five years to assess the progress made so that corrective interventions can then be made.

In fact, it would be more appropriate to describe it as a 'Twenty Five Year Multi-level Action Plan'. The significance of 'Multi-level' becomes apparent when we focus on the how – how will it achieve.

Let us say each year Z number of babies are born in the Nation. We have to cater to all the babies. There is no way that this can be done in the first year of the Plan. Let us say to cater to 20 babies we need one individual who will inspire the 20 babies. We then need Z/20 = Y number of inspirers.

Please note that those who will cater to the babies are not being called care-givers or Anganwadi workers or Anganwadi helpers or nursery teachers but they must be known as inspirers since that is the crux of the catering to be provided to the babies.

Let us call these Y inspirers as level-one inspirers, that is, Inspirers-L1. Where will these Y number of Inspires-L1 come from? They will have to be trained. Who will train them? They will be trained by level-two inspirers, that is, Inspirers-L2. Let us say each Inspirer-L2 can each year train 30 Inspirers-L1. So we will need Y/30 = X number of Inspirers-L2. Inspirers-L2 will be trained by Inspirers-L3 and they in turn by Inspirers-L4, etc.

Clearly we need a new service – Indian Service of Inspirers, our very own and unique ISI.

In the first year some new-born babies will have Inspirers-L1 to cater to them. Some Inspirers-L2 will be there to train more Inspirers-L1 etc. New programmes will have to be established to hasten the process of training each level of Inspirers. The system will initially have to be designed to be accelerative each successive year and then slow down until a steady-state situation is achieved. Clearly this sounds complicated nevertheless it can be designed readily for we have many who will model this with mathematical skills and produce a comprehensive plan.

Creating the necessary infrastructure that is buildings, play facilities and providing learning resources that is toys, flashcard, jigsaw puzzles etc. would also have to planned and provided. All this too can be organized. What may be most difficult to organize will be to find people who can be interested to become Inspirers. People will have to be attracted to join the ISI.

This service, the Indian Service of Inspirers, ISI, must not be treated at par but better than school teachers, college teachers, better than the Indian Administrative Service, IAS, the Indian Foreign Service, IFS, the Indian Police Service, IPS etc. with better remuneration and perks. Only then will Inspiring be viewed as a worthwhile profession and Inspirers will get the respect that they deserve. Only then there will be an incentive for inidividuals to seek a position in the ISI.

So that the Inspirers can do their job and do it well, their work must not be overseen by the bureaucracy, the bureaucrats will not be able to stomach that Inspirers of the ISI are given more respect, remuneration and perks than them. The Inspirers will not be positioned in any Ministry of the Government–central or state. They will be inspired to do their work to the best of their abilities, abilities which will be developed to a very high standard by the SENOG Delivery Commission (SDC). The SDC shall be created by an Act of Parliament and given not only total functional autonomy but also financial autonomy.

The Act shall specify that X percent (X to be worked out by educational, industrial, engineering and management experts) of the budgets of the center and each state shall automatically be given to the SDC. No government, no party in power, no one shall have any authority to alter X.

The SDC will consist of 12 members along with the President of India who shall be its Chairperson. All the 12 members shall be of the highest repute: 2 Inspirers, 2 educationists, 2 industrialists, 2 engineers, 2 management professionals and 2 philanthropists. Initially, one of each of these six categories will be for appointed for 5 years and the other six for 10 years. After 5 years, when 6 members complete their terms, their positions will be filled by 6 who shall be appointed for 10 years so that thereafter every five years one member from each of the six categories will retire and the other six will continue along with 6 new appointees.

Members of the SDC shall have a rank equivalent to that of a Cabinet Minister of the Central Government. They will be appointed by the President after he/she invites nominations from 24 individuals, that is, from 4 well known professionals of each category that he identifies by seeking information from relevant professional societies. The selection committee shall consist of 6 experts, one of each category, randomly selected from the 24 who were invited to send in the nominations and shall be chaired by the Vice President of India. Political parties and the government shall have no say at all in the nomination/selection process. It will be observed that the process outlined above is an attempt to ensure that there is no lobbying possible for selecting members of the SDC. It can certainly be fine tuned further so that only the best of the best become members of the SDC and we can then count on their commitment to ensure that the SENOG Delivery Commission actually delivers.

And I believe it can all be done so long as we have the resolve. To help generate this resolve is the purpose of this Book. It will take much more than just a book to see that resolve take form. But so long as this Book helps in that endeavour, it will have served its purpose.

Let us finally respond to our babies' request for Gimme Five and give them the five, the SENOG, with loads of zeal and zest – they deserve it and only then will our babies when they grow up be able to give us what we all pine for – an *achha yug*.

Index

About the Book

On the basis of ample evidence:

the author suggests that the Gimme Five needed by children aged 0-6 years is SENOG

S – Security endowed with love and care
E – Environment that is clean and hygenic
N – Nutrition through appropriate food
O – Opportunity to explore and engage in a vast variety of activities
G – Guidance that ensures appropriate nurturing

Read about SENOG, ponder over it, and then let us provide it to all our youngest citizens.

*****

On the basis of logic:

the author suggests that we can make India the best country in the world by facilitating provision of SENOG to all our youngest citizens and to accomplish this, the Nation needs to establish its very own and unique ISI, that is the, Indian Service of Inspirers.

Read about ISI, ponder over it and then promote the idea so that it becomes a reality and in a few generations India will lead the world.

About the Author

Shashi K. Gulhati is an engineer-educationist. He graduated from MIT, USA and returned to India to join the faculty of IIT Delhi (IITD) from where he retired about a dozen years ago after serving for 40 years – 28 as Professor. He served as Head of Civil Engineering, as Dean of Students, as a member of IITD's Board of Governors. A highly regarded professional, he served as a member of AICTE and President of the Indian Geotechnical Society. On leave from IITD, he served as the CEO of Educational Consultants India Ltd. (EdCIL) – a Government of India enterprise and transformed it into an efficient, professional, service oriented organization. EdCIL's turnover increased multi-fold during his 5-year term. He has worked internationally as an engineer, an academician and also as an educational consultant. Currently, he consults and enjoys writing on issues in Education – his book on *The IITs Slumping or Soaring*, Macmillan 2007 has been highly acclaimed.